GLOBETROTTER™

Travel G

VENICE

LINDSAY HUNT

*** Highly recommended
** Recommended
* See if you can

First edition published in 2001
by New Holland Publishers (UK) Ltd
London • Cape Town • Sydney • Auckland
10 9 8 7 6 5 4 3 2 1

Garfield House, 86 Edgware Road
London W2 2EA
United Kingdom

80 McKenzie Street
Cape Town 8001
South Africa

14 Aquatic Drive
Frenchs Forest NSW2086
Australia

218 Lake Road, Northcote
Auckland
New Zealand

Distributed in the USA by
The Globe Pequot Press
Connecticut

ISBN 1 85974 830 9

Manager Globetrotter Maps: John Loubser
Managing Editor: Thea Grobbelaar
Editor: Thea Grobbelaar
Design and DTP: Lellyn Creamer
Cartographer: Elaine Fick
Picture Researcher: Colleen Abrahams
Consultant: Tracey Gambarotta
Proofreader: Claudia dos Santos
Indexer: Melany McCallum
Reproduction by Hirt & Carter (Pty) Ltd, Cape Town
Printed and bound in Hong Kong by Sing Cheong Printing Co. Ltd.

Acknowledgements:
The author would like to thank the Italian tourist authorities in London and Venice; Go Airlines and Time Off Ltd for help with travel and accommodation arrangements; the Venice in Peril Fund, and the owners and staff of museums, churches, hotels and places of interest in Venice (too numerous to list) who gave her their time and advice.

Photographic Credits:
Axiom/Steve J. Benbow: page 77;
Axiom/Lucy Davies: page 97;
Axiom/James Morris: pages 41, 90;
Axiom/Luke White: page 64;
Mark Azavedo Photo Library: pages 10, 35, 27, 28, 46, 56, 61, 86, 87, 88, 89, 96, 98;
Mark Azavedo Photo Library/Pam Ainsley: title page, pages 18, 81;
SCPL: page 23;
SCPL/Gill Dishart: pages 13, 101;
SCPL/Peter Dishart: page 9;
SCPL/David W. Gibbons: pages 24, 51, 99;
SCPL/J. Murdock: page 66;
SCPL/Jonathan Smith: page 6;
SCPL/Monika Smith: page 68;
GI/TS/Oliver Ben: page 106;
GI/TS/Ken Fisher: page 19;
GI/TS/Gavin Hellier: page 114;
GI/TS/Simeone Huber: page 34;
GI/TS/Wilfried Krecichwost: page 109;
Lindsay Hunt: pages 40, 60, 62, 63, 65, 71, 82, 83, 105;
The Hutchison Library: page 12;
The Hutchison Library/K. Rodgers: page 26;
The Hutchison Library/Tony Souter: page 107;
Caroline Jones: pages 14, 53, 70, 72, 93;
PhotoBank/Jeanetta Baker: pages 100, 112;
PhotoBank/Peter Baker: pages 15, 20, 39, 78, 110, 111, 113;
PhotoBank/Gary Goodwin: page 94;
Richard Sale: pages 4, 49, 50, 58, 102, 108;
Neil Setchfield: pages 29, 33, 36, 45, 52;
Robin Smith: cover, pages 7, 17, 22, 25, 30, 37, 42, 95;
Jeroen Snijders: pages 21, 47, 54, 59, 74, 75, 76, 84, 85;
SCPL = Sylvia Cordaiy Photo Library;
GI/TS = Gallo Images/Tony Stone

Cover: *A gondola glides past San Giorgio Maggiore.*
Title Page: *Carnival masks are a feature of Venice.*

CONTENTS

1
Introducing Venice

A Byzantine skyline of bubbling domes and tilting bell towers, fading palazzi mirrored in shimmering canals, gondolas skimming across the water … so well documented is Venice that no traveller can arrive without a suitcase full of preconceptions. The strange thing is that while Venice looks exactly as expected, it remains eternally mysterious and alluring. The existence of such an improbably beautiful place, apparently floating on the water line, seems almost miraculous. Part of the magic is the sensation that it could all vanish in the blink of an eye, like some lost Atlantis. Sadly, this is no idle fantasy. The current threats to Venice from environmental change are very real indeed.

'We fear no invasion or seizure by the kings or princes of this world … unless they come by sea,' the Venetians said to the Byzantine Emperor Longinus, on his state visit to their new city in the mid-6th century AD. With barbarians hard on their heels, those early settlers found sanctuary behind their sea moat on a spongy archipelago at the head of the Adriatic. Fifteen hundred years on, it is the sea that presents the greatest challenge to Venice's long-term future.

La Serenissima's glory days as a great sea power and an independent city-state may be over, but nowhere else can claim such artistic and architectural treasures combined with such a beguiling setting. Millions of visitors annually dwarf its resident population of less than 60,000, lower now than at any time since the Black Death. Today, Venice struggles to combine two conflicting roles – world-class tourist attraction and the modern capital of one of Europe's most prosperous and dynamic economic regions.

Top Attractions

*** **Basilica di San Marco:** one of the world's most exotic and richly decorated churches.
*** **Palazzo Ducale:** a *tour de force* of Gothic architecture.
*** **Accademia:** essential visiting for anyone interested in Venetian painting.
*** **Grand Canal:** offers the grandest introduction to the city's palatial architecture.
*** **Rialto:** famous bridge and ancient market zone.
*** **Lagoon:** take a tour of some of the outlying islands – Torcello, Murano or Burano.
*** **Scuola Grande di San Rocco:** décor by Tintoretto.

Opposite: *The domes of the Basilica di San Marco, seen from the Campanile.*

CLIMATE

Venice has a more varied and extreme climate than its Mediterranean location suggests. Rainfall is fairly high most of the year, and summer thunderstorms can produce sudden deluges. Summers can be very humid and oppressive, winters exceptionally chilly. Visibility may be affected by haze in hot weather (sunlight reacts with air pollution from the industrial mainland) and sea fogs add a mournful touch in winter. Temperatures are modified by winds like the *bora* (a cold easterly air stream from the Adriatic), or the *sirocco* (a hot, sultry wind from North Africa). Between October and March, *acque alte* (surge tides) are likely. May–Jun and Sep–Oct generally have the best weather; the wettest months are April and November.

THE LAND

'Land' is a strange concept to use in a city almost entirely defined by water. The land area of the island city, or ***centro storico***, covers a mere 7km^2 (2.7 sq miles) but the entire ***comune***, or municipality, of Venice also encompasses the ***estuario*** or outlying lagoon islands – another 50km^2 (19.3 sq miles) of land area – and a sizeable chunk of the mainland or ***terra firma*** too (134km^2/51.7 sq miles). This includes the industrialized centres of Mestre, Marghera and Chioggia. Over half of Greater Venice's administrative area consists of water belonging to its lagoon and canals. Inland lies the **Veneto**, one of Italy's wealthiest regions, extending to the Dolomite Mountains, the eastern shores of Lake Garda and the historic cities of Verona, Vicenza and Padua. The Veneto has seven provinces, including **Venezia** (Venice) itself.

The Lagoon

Venice occupies a unique lagoon setting near the Po Delta in northeastern Italy. The city is built on a cluster of low-lying islands interlaced by a maze of bridges and canals, and linked to *terra firma* by an artificial causeway carrying road and rail connections. The shallow, dish-like lagoon is partly protected from the open Adriatic by a natural breakwater of slender sand bars reinforced by sea walls. Three openings allow shipping in and out, as well as the twice-daily tides which scour the basin of its debris, salinate its waters, and periodically inundate its islands, which rise less than a metre above the water line. Navigable routes marked by lines of wooden pylons (*bricole*) weave along ancient river beds through the mud banks of the lagoon, which extends approximately 50km (30 miles) at its longest point, and varies in width between 8km (5 miles) and 15km (9 miles). Some of the rivers that once flowed into the lagoon from the mainland have been canalized and diverted directly into the open sea.

Below: *Torri del Benaco, Lake Garda.*

Those that still lead into it bear heavy loads of silt and toxic waste. Constant dredging is necessary to maintain deep-water shipping channels for the supertankers en route to the mainland petro-chemical refineries at Porto Marghera.

Above: *The Grand Canal is one of the most majestic waterways in the world.*

The Island City

The single most striking feature on a map of Venice's *centro storico*, or historic quarter, is the inverted S-bend of the **Grand Canal**, swooping through the city's heart like some Medieval heraldic device. This is the city's main highway, stretching from the broad basin of St Mark's up to the railway station and mainland bridge at its northern end. Central Venice is divided into separate districts called *sestieri* (sixths), three on either side of the Canal. The eastern sector of this six-piece jigsaw consists of **San Marco**, **Castello** and **Cannaregio**; to the west are **Santa Croce**, **San Polo** and **Dorsoduro**. The Canal makes a useful navigational aid, but is bridged at only three points, so plan your sightseeing accordingly.

Most of the big tourist attractions lie in San Marco (**St Mark's Square** with the **Basilica**, **Doge's Palace** and **Campanile**), San Polo (**Rialto Bridge** and **markets**, **Frari church** and **Scuola Grande di San Rocco**), and Dorsoduro (**Accademia** and **Peggy Guggenheim Collection**). Boundaries between the *sestieri* are obvious only on a map (*see* page 8), but each has a subtly different character. The unsung, hidden corners are just as memorable and enjoyable as the crowded main sights, so curiosity pays handsome dividends if you have time to explore. A detailed town plan is essential, though few cities can have changed so little over the centuries as historic Venice. Titian or Canaletto could still show you around without much difficulty.

Fact File

- Number of islands: 118
- Number of bridges: 400
- Number of canals: 170
- Total extent of canals: 44km (27 miles)
- Total extent of streets: 200km (125 miles)
- Area of island city: similar to New York's Central Park
- Mean height above sea level: 80cm (31.5 in)
- Highest point (Campanile di San Marco): 98.5m (323ft)
- Resident population of historic city: 57,000, and falling
- Workers involved in the tourist industry: 50 per cent
- Population of the Veneto: 4.5 million
- Cost of living: 3 per cent higher than Rome
- Average annual income: lowest in the Veneto.

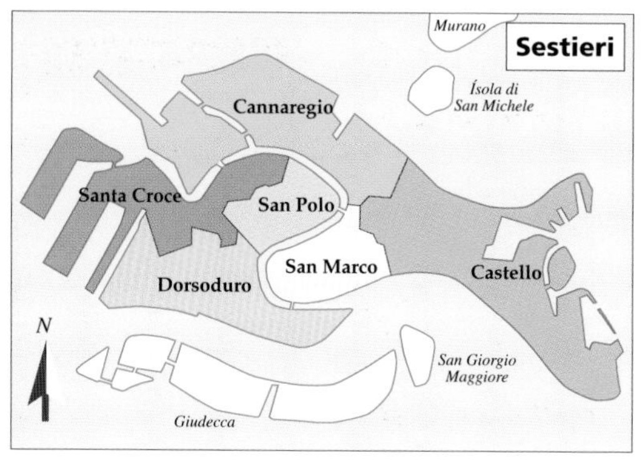

HISTORY IN BRIEF

Venice has a very precise birthday. It officially came into existence at noon on 25 March in AD421, making it (at the time of writing) 1579 years, eight months, six days, four hours and 55 minutes old! But this is a little disingenuous. When the first footsteps were taken on Venetian soil is impossible to know. Small communities of wandering 'fisher-gatherers' probably roamed around the lagoon for centuries before Christ was born, but the city's true history began only with the decline and fall of the Roman Empire.

Earliest Times

Roman **Venetia** (the present Veneto) was a flourishing and wealthy place full of thriving colonies like Padua, Verona and Vicenza. But the marshy islands scattered across the lagoon offered few attractions, and were left more or less deserted. By the 4th century AD, Pax Romana was beginning to come apart at the seams, and in a last-ditch attempt to regain control, the Empire was split into two sections. The eastern dominions were governed from a new centre – **Byzantium**, later known as **Constantinople** (now the city of Istanbul). The Western Empire under Roman rule continued to crumble. For the next two centuries hostile invaders poured through northern Italy to pick at the spoils, including Goths, Lombards and, most ferocious of all, **Attila the Hun**. Successive waves of refugees fled the mainland cities and sought safe havens on the lagoon islands, where the barbarian horsemen could not follow. With them they brought the culture and civilization of the Classical age, and slowly began to rebuild their lives. The lagoon's abundant stocks of fish and salt provided not only a means of survival, but valuable trading commodities.

MANNING THE GALLEYS

Venice's naval supremacy over the Adriatic during the Renaissance was achieved with the perfection of the swift, highly organized **trireme**, an oared galley manned by crews of up to 150. The oarsmen were arranged in groups of three, each led by a foreman, and kept in time by a drummer who sat on the stern. Conditions aboard were cramped and harsh; many crews were made up of prisoners commuting their sentences with a spell in the galleys. Enemy ships were attacked by bow-mounted cannon and a pointed battering ram on the prow. Sails could be hoisted for a swift getaway. The last great sea battle fought with oared galleys was at Lepanto in 1571, when Venice led a successful attack on the Turks. **The Museo Storico Navale** contains a fine model of a trireme.

The islanders at first looked to the Eastern Empire for their protection, but soon began to chafe against their foreign yoke. They elected a **doge** (the Venetian word for *duce*, meaning leader, from the Latin *dux*) to represent their interests against Byzantine whims.

In AD752, the lagoon settlers faced another serious threat of invasion, this time from the Franks under Charlemagne's son, **Pepin**. To defend themselves more easily, the scattered communities withdrew from the outer islands like Torcello to the **Rivus Altus** (Rialto), high and dry in the centre of the lagoon. Pepin's deep-draughted siege ships were craftily lured into the shallows, where they foundered on the sandbanks, and their helpless crews were massacred.

Glowing with newfound confidence after this maritime triumph, Venice began a much more organized and centralized existence, developing trade links with the East, securing shipping routes against pirates, and establishing a powerful seat of government in the Rialto islands under its doges. Gradually it coalesced into **Civitas Venetiarum**, an independent city-state under the auspices of the Byzantine Empire. One single event crystallized Venice's sense of nationhood more than any other – the theft of the relics of **St Mark** from Alexandria in AD828. The previous patron of the city (St Theodore, a shadowy Byzantine imposition) was summarily demoted, and the Lion of the Evangelist began to roar in every corner of the Adriatic.

THE LION OF ST MARK

All over Venice and the cities of the Veneto, lions appear on pillars, plinths, parapets, walls, tombs, gates and bridges. The **winged lion** is the symbol of St Mark, an appropriately regal beast to represent the might of the Most Serene Republic. Many lion monuments hold a paw on an open book revealing the Latin inscription: *Pax tibi, Marce, Evangelista meus* (Peace unto you, Mark, my Evangelist). These were the words of an angel appearing to St Mark in a dream, predicting that his body would one day lie in Venice. The lion on the gates of the Arsenale naval dockyards, however, holds a closed book, implying a more belligerent stance.

Below: *St Mark's winged lions decorate monuments all over the city.*

The Crusading Years

The year 1000 was a significant one for the Venetians. Under **Doge Pietro Orseolo**, one of the Republic's most skilful leaders, rebel bases on the Dalmatian coast were

finally overthrown, and important trading outposts were brought under Venetian control. This victory is commemorated in the 'Marriage to the Sea' ceremony, still remembered annually on the Lido. The seafaring **Dalmatians** honed Venice's shipbuilding skills, enabling it to expand its influence in the southern Adriatic, and become the dominant partner in the Byzantine Empire. In 1082, in gratitude for Venice's help against the Normans (another major Mediterranean sea power), the Byzantine emperor granted Venetian merchants exemption from all taxes and duties, a huge boost to the Republic's growing prosperity. The invaluable trading routes to the Orient now lay firmly in Venice's sights, a commercial advantage it exploited with ruthless determination.

Venice's next great opportunity for advancement came with the **First Crusade** in 1095. While playing no prominent military role, the city agreed to supply ships and equipment for the vast army of adventure-seekers who blazed their way through Europe and the Byzantine Empire to wrest the Holy Land from the Muslims. Despite claiming the moral high ground on behalf of the Christian world, Venice's motivation in this shrewd arms-dealing exercise was in fact primarily financial.

The huge rewards that the city demanded from the crusading armies proved too onerous, and by the time of the **Fourth Crusade** in 1202, the Christian leaders had run out of funds. Venice struck a deal to settle the debt. The price was the city to which it owed not only its political allegiance, but a large part of its economic success – **Constantinople**. In 1204, on a somewhat flimsy pretext of uniting the Orthodox and Catholic wings of the Church, the Crusaders brutally sacked the Byzantine capital, slaughtering thousands of its Christian inhabitants in the process. The Venetians then carried off the fabulous spoils of their erstwhile

KEEPING IT IN THE FAMILY

Many great names in Venetian art apply to more than one person. Families worked together, fathers passing skills to children. An early dynasty was the **Bellini** family, consisting of Jacopo and his sons Gentile and Giovanni. Andrea **Mantegna** married into this family. *Quattrocento* (1400s) contemporaries included the **Vivarini** family – Antonio, brother Bartolomeo and son Alvise. After the death of Paolo **Veronese**, his brother and son carried on his work, signing themselves 'Paolo's heirs'. Jacopo **Tintoretto's** sons Domenico and Marco, and a daughter Marietta, inherited their father's talent, as did Giandomenico **Tiepolo**, following his more famous father Giambattista. So artists must be distinguished by their full names, not just surnames. To complicate things further, studio assistants and pupils took on the mantles (and sometimes the signatures) of their mentors.

Historical Calendar

5th–6th centuries AD Settlers arrive on the lagoon islands, fleeing barbarian hordes.
453 Attila the Hun ravages northern Italy.
810 Pepin, son of Charlemagne, conquers Venetia but is defeated by the island city.
828 The body of St Mark is brought to Venice from Alexandria. Work begins on the Basilica.
800–1000 Venice expands her trading empire in the Eastern Mediterranean.
1095 Venice provides ships and supplies for the First Crusade.
1171 The six *sestieri* are established.
1173 The first Rialto Bridge is built.
1204 Sack of Constantinople in the Fourth Crusade; Venice acquires the spoils of the Byzantine Empire, including four bronze horses.
1269 Marco Polo leaves Venice on his Oriental voyages.
1310 Venice formalizes its constitution, and appoints the Council of Ten.
1348 The Black Death halves the population.
1380 Victory over the Genoese at Chioggia assures Venice's naval supremacy in the Mediterranean.
1405 Venice takes Verona, Padua and Vicenza from Milan, and in so doing consolidates its mainland empire.
1453 The Turks conquer Constantinople for the Ottoman Empire.
1498 Vasco da Gama discovers the Cape of Good Hope route to the East Indies, thereby weakening Venice's hold on the spice trade.
1571 The Turks are defeated at the Battle of Lepanto, but Venice loses Cyprus, and later also Crete.
1577 and **1630** Plague outbreaks devastate the city. The Redentore and Salute churches are built.
1718 The loss of Morea to the Turks marks the end of Venice's maritime empire.
1797 Napoleon invades. The last doge abdicates and the Venetian Republic comes to an end.
1815 Napoleon is defeated; Venice and the Veneto are ceded to Austria at the Congress of Vienna.
1848 Daniele Manin leads an unsuccessful revolt against Austrian rule.
1866 The Prussians defeat Austria, and Venice joins a united Italy.
1895 The first Biennale art exhibition takes place.
1902 The Campanile in St Mark's Square collapses.
1920s–30s Massive expansion of Mestre and Marghera as industrialized ports.
1932 The first International Film Festival, and the construction of the Ponte della Libertà road bridge.
1966 Devastating floods wreak havoc in Venice. A huge international rescue effort begins.
1983 Extraction of artesian water is halted; Venice officially stops sinking, but sea levels keep rising.
1988 Work begins on the lagoon sea defences known as MOSE, but ceases a decade later after environmental objections.
1996 The Fenice opera house is destroyed in an arson attack.
2000 Many historic buildings are renovated to mark the millennium. Protests are held after yet more flooding of the city centre.

masters, treasures that had been accumulated over some 900 years. Besides material possessions (including the magnificent team of **bronze chariot horses** from the Hippodrome, which now stand in St Mark's Basilica), Venice also gained most of the Byzantine Empire's territories. These included the Peloponnese and several of the Greek islands, plus a chain of trading posts stretching from the Black Sea to China and the Indies. The conquest of Byzantium was, by any standards, a rather cynical and treacherous manoeuvre but, at least in the short term, a highly profitable one.

Opposite: *Distinctive scroll shapes buttress the domes of Santa Maria della Salute, near the entrance to the Grand Canal.*

Right: *The original bronze horses of St Mark's now stand protected from the elements inside the Basilica museum.*

FAMOUS DOGES

- **Orso Ipato** (726–737), one of the very first doges, drove the Lombards from Ravenna. But for his attempt to make the office of the doge hereditary, he had his throat cut.
- **Angelo Partecipazio** (811–827), whose cunning naval tactics defeated the Franks, moved Venice's capital to the Rialto islands, and built the first Ducal Palace.
- **Enrico Dandolo** (1192–1205), blind and in his 80s, led the Fourth Crusade in the attack on Constantinople.
- **Marin Falier** (1354–1355), a disgraced doge accused of plotting to overthrow the Republic, was beheaded on the steps of the Ducal Palace.
- **Giovanni Mocenigo** (1478–1485) and **Leonardo Loredan** (1501–1521) were immortalized in superb portraits by the Bellini family, while **Pietro Mocenigo** (1474–1476) and **Nicolò Marcello** (1473–1474) were given magnificent tombs by Pietro Lombardo.
- **Sebastiano Venier** (1577–1578) was Commander of the Fleet at the Battle of Lepanto.
- **Francesco Morosini** (1688–1694) recaptured many of Venice's lost possessions (lost again by his successors).
- **Ludovico Manin** (1789–1797) was the last of Venice's doges. He is buried in Cannaregio's Scalzi church.

The Maritime Empire

Venice was now a world player, an imperialist power rather than a trading city. After recovering from the **Black Death** (1348–49), when some 60 per cent of the population was wiped out, it continued its expansionist policies. Over the next two centuries, it concentrated its attention on outpacing seafaring rivals such as **Pisa** and **Genoa**. Besides guarding its interests on the high seas, it also had to watch its back. In order to trade with northern Europe, Venice needed to secure strategic waterways and mountain passes through the mainland **Veneto**, where ambitious dynastic families like the Milanese Visconti and Verona's Scaligeri were very powerful. Through political intrigue and complex alliances it achieved these aims, and by the early 15th century Venice had borders reaching the Alpine foothills and a fleet unequalled anywhere in the Mediterranean.

Realizing the only way from the top is down, wise **Doge Tommaso Mocenigo** counselled against further expansion. But greed got the better of his successors, and while possessions piled up in Venice's imperial coffers (Ravenna, Cremona, Bergamo), the price of acquiring them grew higher. Mercenary generals (*condottieri*) demanded their cut, while the European neighbours who should have been allies grew more jealous of Venice's success.

Decline and Fall

In 1453, an ominous portent came when Constantinople fell to the **Ottoman Turks**, who were rapidly expanding their influence in the eastern Mediterranean. Meanwhile, new horizons of wealth and trade potential were opening up in the Americas, and falling into other colonial hands. In 1498, **Vasco da Gama's** voyage round the Cape of Good Hope rendered the expensive overland route from the Orient (via Venice's customs posts) obsolete overnight. As if this was not enough, a concerted alliance called the **League of Cambrai**, led by the Pope and the Holy Roman Emperor Maximilian, set most of Europe against Venice's thirst for domination. Under Venetian leadership, the western allies won a significant victory against the Turks at **Lepanto** in 1571 (the last major naval battle fought with oared galleys), but after that Venice began to lose her possessions in a steady process of attrition.

Closer to home, too, friction continued; clashes with the Vatican resulted in a Papal Interdict in 1609 excommunicating the entire city. Spying a chance to gain from Venice's troubles, the Spanish and Austrian **Habsburgs** incited uprisings in its few remaining colonies. The Turks renewed their assault, and by 1718, virtually all Venice's Mediterranean territory had been lost.

If Venice was no longer a world power, she was still an important provider of financial services, and the darling of drawing-room society. Venetian art, architecture and music flourished as never before in the years of political decline from the 15th to the 18th centuries. Churches and palaces sprang up all over the city. Grand Tour aesthetes flocked to Venice for improving doses of Palladio and Tintoretto, while spendthrifts and libertines poured to the gaming tables of the Ridotto as well as the newly opened coffee houses of San Marco. In 1790, the **Fenice** opera house opened to delight audiences with the comic antics of Harlequin and Columbine.

Building the City

To create a solid base for Venice's densely packed buildings, billions of wooden stakes cut from the forests of the Dolomites were floated down to the lagoon on rafts. These were driven through the mud into the clay and gravel below. Layers of Istrian marble were placed on top of the wooden piles to support the bridges, towers, palaces and churches, and keep out the damp. The anaerobic, waterlogged subsoil virtually halted the process of decay, which is why these ancient foundations have lasted for so many centuries.

Below: *The Tetrarchs of Diocletian, on the Basilica's south face.*

Gondolas

Part of the city's mythology, the elegant gondola is built to a precise design, adapted for Venice's shallow, angular waterways. The flat hull is asymmetrical (wider on the left than the right to enable a single oarsman to maintain a straight course). Handcrafted from eight kinds of wood, a gondola consists of over 280 pieces of timber. Seven coats of black lacquer are applied to the frame. The bows end in an iron *ferro*, a comb-like structure with six prongs said to represent the city's *sestieri*. The walnut rowlock (*forcola*) can hold the beechwood oar in eight different positions. By the 16th century, gondolas had become ornate symbols of wealth, but since 1562 they have all been black by law, their only decorations being a pair of golden seahorses amidships.

In 1797, **Napoleon** goaded the decadent Venetians into providing him with an excuse to declare war. They put up no resistance, which spared the city at least some futile destruction and bloodshed. The Republic's last doge, **Ludovico Manin**, handed his valet his cap of office, saying, 'Take it, I shall not need this again', and La Serenissima slid to an inglorious conclusion under French occupation. Art treasures were crated up for dispatch to Paris, palaces and churches were demolished, and the great shipyards of the Arsenale were systematically wrecked. The much-travelled quadriga horses were led off to another new home on the Champs Elysées.

After Napoleon's defeat at **Waterloo** in 1815, Venice passed into Austrian hands, and remained a **Habsburg** vassal for the next 50 years. The Austrians were loathed. Their stewardship of the city produced improvements, including the mainland rail link, better sea walls and the restoration of some badly dilapidated buildings, but for most Venetians, the 19th century was a miserable time of unprecedented hunger, poverty, disease and humiliation. Over a quarter of the city was reduced to beggary, and even wealthy aristocrats were forced to sell off the family silver. In 1848, **Daniele Manin**, adopting the rebellious spirit of the Risorgimento, staged a heroic but unsuccessful revolt against Austria. This resulted in the world's first aerial bombardment, using missiles carried by balloons. Venice's liberation arrived via Prussian hands. After Bismarck defeated the Austrians at Sadowa, the **Kingdom of United Italy** was formed, which Venice joined in 1866.

Below: *Gondolas ply from the landing stages near the Rialto Bridge.*

Modern Venice

Political unification did not instantly solve the Veneto's chronic economic depression. Emigration continued to drain its more enterprising citizens for the rest of the 19th century, but gradually things began to

improve. Traditional family-run crafts like glass manufacture and lace-making revived, and even ship-building experienced a mild upswing after the opening of the Suez Canal. Tourism brought a new lease of life, and the **Lido** became one of Europe's most glamorous seaside resorts. After World War I, new manufacturing industries mushroomed in the main-land port at **Marghera**. A road link was added across the lagoon, parallel to the existing rail link. Mainland **Mestre** developed as a cheaper and more convenient dormitory town for Venice's workforce, and a large proportion of the population decamped across the lagoon.

Above: *Waterfront streets present an animated scene.*

Venice has an ambivalent attitude to its visitors. Without them, it would be as dead as mutton, yet with them, it feels utterly beleaguered. One weekend in 1989, around 200,000 people poured into the city for a pop concert, causing havoc in St Mark's Square. Many new schemes have been aired to give Venice alternative economic viability. One, aborted after international protests, was a deplorable idea to drain substantial sections of the lagoon in order to build a site for Expo 2000, a millennium trade fair which, it was anticipated, would attract some 45 million visitors to the city. Today, Venice faces rising sea levels with increasing anxiety. Drastic measures are necessary to save it from a watery grave.

In the face of such extreme difficulties, it is easy to overlook the positive side of Venice, which many outsiders embrace as a model community. The absence of cars, eerie at first, soon seems an utter delight rather than an inconvenience. Feet and public transport are just as swift and efficient; even wheelchair users can now get around more easily. If some of Venice's dogs have less than perfect pavement manners, the city is cleaner and freer of litter, vandalism and graffiti than most in Europe. It also has a remarkably low crime rate; you may be overcharged for a gondola ride, but you stand little risk of being knifed in an alley.

WAYS TO ENJOY VENICE

- Take a *vaporetto* down the Grand Canal, with your camera at the ready.
- Stroll through the city's lesser-known districts, exploring byways and backwaters away from the tourist crowds.
- Join in the evening *passeggiata* with an ice cream or apéritif in an open-air café.
- Visit the city's atmospheric *bacari* or *enoteche* (wine bars) for an *ombra* (glass of wine) and *cichetto* (snack).
- Sample the thrill of a gondola for less than the price of a coffee with a *traghetto* hop across the Canal.
- Climb a campanile or two for sensational views.
- Wander through the street markets of the Rialto in the early morning.
- Window-shop at delectable craft and fashion boutiques.
- Try the chocolate cake at Harry's Dolci.
- Hear a concert of Venetian music in a historic setting.
- Pack a picnic for an excursion to Torcello, or one of the Lido's quieter beaches.

Above: *Italy's flag was designed by Napoleon.* **Opposite:** *Two bronze Atlases carry the weight of the world on the weather-vane of the Dogana di Mare (sea customs post).*

GOVERNMENT AND ECONOMY

The Rule of the Doge

Historians differ over the date of the first doge, but certainly by 726 Venice had a leader denoted *primus inter pares* – first among equals. From then until Napoleon redrew the maps of Europe in 1797, 120 successive doges led La Repubblica Serenissima (the Most Serene Republic) to unprecedented heights. The early doges were military leaders who ruled more or less despotically, but gradually the role became more presidential than executive. Nominees were chosen from a small group of the city's leading patrician families; the same surnames recur for centuries – Contarini, Mocenigo, Morosini. They were generally elderly and, of course, exclusively male. The office of the doge was in theory a lifelong post, but the Republic could, in extreme circumstances, force a doge out of office, and not a few had their natural span curtailed. Several were beheaded or had their throats cut, one was thrown to dogs, others were ritually blinded over hot coals.

Riots followed a 10th-century attempt by one doge to make his position hereditary, and from then on strict rules prevented the doge from exceeding his brief. An amazingly complicated multiple voting system was set up to stop tyrants or conspiritors from influencing elections. Once appointed, the doge was forbidden to meet foreign envoys alone or maintain direct personal links with other heads of state. He was prevented from leaving the city and owning property outside Venice, his mail was scrutinized by censors and the only gifts he could receive were flowers or herbs. No members of his family could hold public office or marry without permission. He received no income, yet had to bear the considerable expenses of his office from his own pocket. Few doges have any memorials in the city other than their tombs. It was a high price to pay for a few moments of pomp and circumstance on Coronation Day, and an annual ride around the lagoon in a gilded barge.

THE MOSES FACTOR

In 1988, work began on a controversial megabillion-lire scheme to place a series of moveable steel dykes at the three entrances to the lagoon to control tidal surges. The project, acronymed MOSE (*Modulo Sperimentale Elettromeccanico*), is aptly enough the Italian name for Moses, that great biblical water engineer. A decade later, the project has been shelved, after strong objections from Venice's Green Party, which fears disastrous side effects on the natural ecosystem of the lagoon and argues that other measures would be more effective. Meanwhile, floods continue, to the exasperation of local residents and businesses, tired of mopping up the mess and paying the bill.

Venetian Institutions

Despite their restricted powers, astute and strong-willed doges could and did wield great influence, and were much more than 'glorified slaves of the Republic', as Petrarch called them. Foreign policy took much concentration; Venice's imperial role meant it was more or less perpetually at war for centuries at a time. But the day-to-day running of the state was carried out by an army of civil servants, and an aristocratic oligarchy of Byzantine complexity was designed to prevent corruption and nepotism. The main legislative body was the **Maggior Consiglio** (Great Council), which grew to around 500 members, whose patrician names were inscribed in a *Libro d'Oro* (Golden Book) from 1315 onwards. The **Senato** and the **Collegio** were inner cabinets with the role of appointing officials and deciding on foreign policy. The **Quarantia** was the main judicial authority. Most feared of all was the **Consiglio dei Dieci**, or Council of Ten, an inquisitorial body which operated in secret with almost unlimited powers. Denunciations, spies and secret police oiled the machinery of the state with terrifying consequences for any citizen who fell foul of it, including the doge himself.

Salt

Venice grew wealthy on the salt trade from the 10th to the 15th centuries. Its great rival in the early days of the Republic was the Po Delta town of Comacchio. In 932 Venice attacked Comacchio and founded its own monopoly on this vital commodity, which brought in a large proportion of its revenue for several hundred years. Most of Venice's salt was panned near Chioggia, though some was imported to control the price. The old Salt Office, which controlled prices and export licences, is now used by a rowing club as a boatyard.

Venice Today

The present government of Venice is very different from the elaborately constituted regime of the Republic, which lasted for over a thousand years. Modern Venice is one of Italy's 20 regional capitals, with a mayor (*sindaco*) as its titular head instead of a doge. Current preoccupations centre on the threat of surge flooding and the rebuilding of the Fenice opera house, rather than the foreign policy of the Ottoman Empire or the state of the spice trade.

SANITARY FACILITIES

In the past, Venice's provision of basic sanitary facilities for its many visitors was lamentable, and sightseeing in the city had to be tailored around visits to bars, restaurants, museums or hotels solely in order to take advantage of their loos. But at long last, the city authorities have grudgingly admitted the existence of a universal need and finally done something to cope (as they put it) 'with the onslaught of tourists'. Dotted all over the city are coin-operated cabins and kiosks marked **AMAV** (*Azienda Multiservizi Ambientali Veneziana*). These cost a fairly princely L1000, but are generally in reasonable condition.

Environmental and conservation issues play an important part in Venetian politics today, though few have escaped the tarnish of financial scandals as money intended for the city's renovation vanished into countless black holes as bribes and slush funds. During the 1990s, the Northern League, led by Umberto Bossi, unsuccessfully campaigned for complete independence of the wealthy regions of the north, who perceive southern Italy and the centralized government of Rome as a corrupt and unproductive hindrance to economic progress. In 1997 one protest group staged a bizarre mini-coup in St Mark's Square, storming the Campanile and declaring a rebirth of the Venetian Republic (before being arrested and imprisoned for disturbing the peace).

Revenue from tourism keeps Venice afloat these days, and also makes a major contribution to the Veneto's booming economy, but many other industries, such as glass, metallurgy, petrochemicals, fashion and textiles, play a vital role too. As elsewhere, economic success has a high price tag. While Venice, scarcely changed for centuries, remains as beautiful as ever, parts of the mainland have been irrevocably spoilt by overdevelopment. The highly polluting industrial plants of Mestre and Marghera produce a whole raft of problems. A noxious brew of sulphurous smog combines with salt and damp to gnaw the stonework of the city, while sewage and phosphate effluent poison the Adriatic's wildlife and seafood, causing bizarre algal blooms from time to time. Many dilemmas face Venice as it struggles to reconcile the demands of a modern urban society with its status as a uniquely precious historic monument. Schemes to prevent flooding, or build a metro system, have been hot topics of debate in the last decade, supporters favouring Venice's modernization, detractors fearing the impact of such radical changes on the city's fragile structure and the ecosystem of its lagoon.

Below: *A colourful example of Murano's many styles of glasswear.*

THE PEOPLE

Above: *Venetian gondoliers are easily recognizable in their traditional costume of beribboned straw boaters and striped shirts.*

True Venetians are an endangered species. Between 12 and 20 million tourists visit Venice annually (many are day-trippers, so precise numbers are hard to assess), but the residents continue to depart. About 1500 people are estimated to leave the city permanently each year, discouraged by the high cost of living and property prices, and the lack of long-term employment except in the tourist industry. Many small businesses have collapsed, and property passes ever more often into the hands of wealthy outsiders than Venetians. A large proportion of the workforce lives on the mainland and commutes over the Ponte della Libertà, leaving an ageing, demographically unbalanced population behind in the *centro storico.* Reversing this trend and making the city a viable option for young people and families to live and work is seen as an urgent priority by the authorities.

The Venetian character is seen in many contradictory ways. Other Italians find them moody and lazy, rebellious and cold. In fact, their history shows they are enterprising, hard-working people, practical at solving the logistics of life without wheels, and astonishingly tolerant of the tourists who relentlessly and often insensitively invade their territory. They are wily and quick-witted, civilized and dignified in manner, and full of civic pride. Adept at making money, they like to spend it too, on stylish clothes and the good things of life. They enjoy relaxing in cafés and bars, and adore the colourful pageantry of carnivals and regattas. Many take regular holidays on the mainland, heading for the Veneto countryside or the Dolomite peaks to escape the 'cabin fever' of their island setting.

Native city-dwellers are perhaps easiest to spot during an *acqua alta* (surge tide), when the lagoon spills over the Riva degli Schiavoni and bubbles up between the paving stones of St Mark's Square. While tourists gawk at the city liquefying beneath their feet, Venetians don designer wellingtons and carry on with everyday life as elegantly as ever, perfectly adapted to this strange waterland.

ICE CREAM

As in other parts of Italy, ice cream is an art form in Venice, and nothing presents such an exquisitely agonizing choice as a counter full of tempting and exotic flavours. You need to specify whether you want a cone (*cono*) or a tub (*coppa*), then choose your scoops (the biggest is often last). Cream (*panna*) may also be offered, but this is gilding the lily. Takeaway prices vary from about L2000 upwards, but be warned: if you choose to sit at a terrace table in a café, the price will be much higher. Some of Venice's most famous *gelaterie* are **Nico** (on the Zattere in Dorsoduro), **Causin** (in Campo Santa Margarita, also in Dorsoduro) and **Paolin** (in Campo Santo Stefano, San Marco).

Above: *There's always a surprise in the streets of Venice, as artists, entertainers and musicians catch the visitor's eye.*

Language

Venessian is the version of Italian spoken in Venice, responsible for those unusual spellings on street signs and menus. Similar forms are spoken throughout the Veneto. Listen for it as gondoliers talk among themselves, at the stalls of the Rialto, or in the bars and cafés of Cannaregio or Castello. The sing-song accent is distinctive – elision producing some odd results. Thus the church of Giovanni e Paolo ends up as Zanipolo, and Sant'Eustachio as San Stae. Some say Venessian (or Venet) is a true language rather than a dialect, and claim it has closer links with its Latin forebear than Dante's Tuscan variant which became standard modern Italian. Venice's colonial past introduced many words from communities as diverse as Greeks, Germans, Dalmatians, Turks, Egyptians, Armenians and Jews.

Chorus

Many of Venice's more interesting churches now charge admission, which goes some way towards their upkeep and restoration. Prices are generally modest, but if you enjoy visiting churches you can save money on multiple entries by buying a **Chorus pass** (currently L15,000), which is valid for 13 splendid churches covered under the Foundation for the Churches of Venice scheme. These include Santa Maria Gloriosa dei Frari, Santa Maria dei Miracoli, Santa Maria Formosa, Redentore, Madonna dell'Orto, San Giacomo dell'Orio, Santo Stefano, San Pietro di Castello, San Polo, San Sebastiano, Santa Maria del Giglio, San Stae and Sant'Alvise. All of these contain beautiful works of art and many fascinating architectural features.

Art

It is a rare Venetian church, however minor, without some Renaissance masterpiece lurking in a darkened side-chapel which a 200-lire coin can transform with dazzling effect. The riches housed in its palazzi, public buildings, museums and galleries could keep art-lovers agog for weeks. Yet what exists now is but a fraction of what the city once had. Huge quantities of art were looted or sold when Napoleon invaded, and when wealthy Venetians faced impoverishment in the 18th and 19th centuries. The trend was partially reversed by the first Biennale exhibition in 1895, which made Venice a world showcase for modern art. In the 20th century, benefactors like Peggy Guggenheim and Baron Franchetti contributed to the city's public art collections.

Close ties with Byzantium influenced Venetian art in the Middle Ages. Mosaics and icons glitter in older churches like the Cathedral of Santa Maria dell'Assunta in Torcello and the Basilica di San Marco. Byzantine craftsmen created the astonishing altar screen in St Mark's (the Pala d'Oro), commissioned by Doge Falier in 1105. Great individualists like the Florentine **Giotto** were at work in the Veneto by the 14th century (his fresco cycle in Padua was completed in 1305). One of the earliest Venetian artists to be known by name was **Paolo Veneziano** (ca. 1321–62), who introduced the polyptych (multi-panelled painting) to the city. The iconographic **Byzantine** style gradually elided with the more decorative approach of **Gothic** art, whose main exponents in the Veneto were **Gentile da Fabriano** (ca. 1370–1427) and **Michele Giambono** (1420–62).

The **Renaissance** produced one of the greatest of all Venetian painters, **Giovanni Bellini** (1430–1516), whose lustrous works illumine the churches of the Frari and San Zaccaria, as well as the Accademia. His father Jacopo and brother Gentile also painted memorable works. Contemporaries included **Andrea Mantegna** (1431–1506), the **Vivarini** family, **Cima da Conegliano** (ca. 1459–1517) and **Vittore Carpaccio** (ca. 1460–1526), whose detailed canvases record a vivid picture of contemporary Venetian life. Architectural settings and clever use of perspectives brought new dimensions to the static quality of earlier styles.

In the 16th century, new oil painting techniques revolutionized the potential for drama and movement. **Lorenzo Lotto** (1480–1556) is famed for his haunting psychological portraits, and **Giorgione** (1475–1510) gained more attention through his enigmatic *Tempest* than most artists achieve with a lifetime's output. Venice's outstanding artists of the **High Renaissance** were **Titian** (1485–1576) and **Tintoretto** (1518–94), whose virtuoso masterpieces can be seen all over the city. **Paolo Veronese** (1528–88) was another prolific painter of huge and dynamic works during this period.

In the 18th century the **Tiepolos** (Giambattista and his son Giandomenico) brought Venetian art into the limelight with their sensual versions of **Rococo** art. Contemporaries like **Francesco Guardi** (1712–93) and **Antonio Canal** (1697–1768), better known as Canaletto, belonged to the rather different genre of *vedutisti* (landscape painters), immortalizing Venice in their 'postcard' scenes.

Veneto Wines

The Veneto is an important wine-producing region. Familiar names include red Bardolino and Valpolicella, and the undemanding white Soave. More interesting labels are Bianco di Custoza and Pinot Grigio, or the white Tocai wines from the Friuli district. House wines are light, fruity Merlots or Cabernets, while Prosecco is a sparkling wine in various grades of sweetness, often drunk as an apéritif. Dessert wines include the fortified red Recioto Amarone, and the sweet white Gambarella. Venice is noted for cocktails and liqueurs too. A popular typical apéritif is a spritzer, made with white wine, seltzer or soda and an astringent additive such as Campari or Aperol. The classic after-dinner grappa is a clear, fiery spirit distilled from grape skins.

Below: *A typically avant-garde work on display in the Biennale art exhibition.*

Cover Up

There's a dress code in Venetian churches. Shorts, revealing tops and skirts above the knee are strictly prohibited, particularly in the Basilica. No tanktops, no strappy sundresses. If you are considered improperly dressed you may not be allowed to enter. Visitors are also reminded to remain silent, behave discreetly, and not to take photographs inside the building. Sightseeing is not allowed during services, though you can stand quietly at the back or sides of the church and enter and leave at some suitable interval.

Architecture

Venice is a giant open-air museum of monumental buildings, many in a parlous state with unstable foundations, eroding stonework and chronic rising damp. Churches and palaces stand shrouded in protective sheeting, swallowing vast quantities of restorative conservation funds.

Architectural styles are Byzantine, Romanesque, Gothic, Renaissance, Palladian and Baroque. Despite ideas from all over its vast trading empire, Venice's buildings manage by osmosis to gel into something distinctively Venetian. The façades along the Grand Canal belong nowhere else.

Torcello Cathedral is considered the oldest surviving building in the city. Dating from around AD1008, it has many **Byzantine** features. Venice's best-known example of Byzantine style is the **Basilica di San Marco**. Churches display variations of the basilica pattern – a covered hall flanked by colonnaded aisles – originally used in Greek and Roman buildings. The Byzantine style of the 12th–13th centuries can be seen in some of Venice's early palaces too, such as the **Palazzo Loredan** or the **Fondaco dei Turchi**.

The most typical feature of the **Veneto-Gothic** style is the **ogee arch**, an idiosyncratic combination of concave and convex shapes, often embellished with trefoil or quatrefoil (clover-leaf) tracery and Moorish minarets, reaching its apogee in the **Palazzo Ducale** and the **Ca' d'Oro**.

Renaissance buildings from the 15th century mark a return to **Classical** architecture, with harmonious proportions. Architects, rather than their patrons, become individually known. Renaissance architects whose work can be seen in Venice include Florentine **Jacopo Sansovino** (1486–1570), Veronese **Michele Sanmicheli** (1484–1559), and sculptor **Pietro Lombardo** (1435–1515). The greatest was Paduan master **Andrea Palladio** (1508–80), most of whose public buildings and villas lie around Vicenza and in the Brenta Valley. He is widely held to be the most influential architect of all time.

Below: *A Palladian masterpiece – Villa Barbaro at Maser near Asolo.*

Music

Above: *Music is a regular form of entertainment in Piazza San Marco.*

The first renowned composer associated with Venice was **Andrea Gabrieli** (born there in 1510), later organist at St Mark's. He wrote large-scale choral and orchestral works and madrigals. **Monteverdi** (1567–1643) was not a native Venetian, but became musical director at St Mark's in 1613, where he devoted himself mostly to church music, and wrote several of the first great modern operas, including *Orfeo*. **Albinoni** (1671–1750), an accomplished Baroque composer, was overshadowed by his prolific contemporary **Vivaldi** (1678–1741), who wrote concerti by the barrowload (*see* panel). The opening of the **Fenice opera house** in 1790 was another landmark in Venice's musical success. In the 19th century, the great romantic composers **Wagner**, **Verdi** and **Rossini** all set operas in Venice, and the tradition continued into the 20th; Britten's *Turn of the Screw* and Stravinsky's *The Rake's Progress* were both premiered in the city.

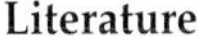

Literature

Venice has inspired countless literary works. **Dante** set scenes from *The Inferno* in the shipyards of the Arsenale, and **Petrarch** wrote many love sonnets while living on the Riva degli Schiavoni. **Shakespeare** never visited Venice, but brought the 16th-century Rialto vividly to life in *The Merchant of Venice*. From then on, any well-travelled writer felt obliged to soak up some Venetian atmosphere at some stage. Poets **Wordsworth**, **Byron** and **Shelley** developed strong associations with the city, along with **Goethe**, **Proust**, **Henry James**, **Thomas Mann** and many other writers. Relatively few native Venetian writers are well known outside Italy, but the name of playwright **Carlo Goldoni** (1707–93, *see* panel, page 77) lives on in theatrical circles, while **Marco Polo** and **Casanova** are remembered for their voluminous but very different memoirs – of oriental travel and steamy seduction.

The Red Priest

Antonio Vivaldi, nicknamed *il prete rosso* because of his red hair, devoted much of his life to teaching music at the orphanage for girls attached to La Pietà church. From 1703 to 1740, he taught the violin and ran the choir, besides finding time to write many of his finest pieces. The music school became so famous that some ambitious parents tried to secure a place for their offspring by pretending they were foundlings. Vivaldi's style eventually fell out of favour (unkind critics said he wrote the same concerto 454 times), and he left Venice to die penniless in Vienna soon afterwards. Today, Venice treats him with more respect.

Film

The first **international film festival**, held on the Lido in 1932, brought Venice into sharp focus with cinema-goers. Since then, this photogenic city has enjoyed bit parts and backdrop roles in thousands of films. Cinematic versions of *Othello* or *Casanova* naturally demanded Venetian settings. Hollywood mock-ups were used for *Trouble in Paradise* (1932) and the musical *Top Hat* (1935). *Three Coins in the Fountain* (1954) was another lighthearted look at the city. More recent films have penetrated the darker depths of melancholy and horror, notably in screenings of novels by Thomas Mann (*Death in Venice*, 1971), Ian McEwan (*The Comfort of Strangers*, 1990), and Daphne du Maurier (*Don't Look Now*, 1973). The Henry James period classics *The Wings of the Dove* and *The Portrait of a Lady* have had a Merchant Ivory make-over with glossy location shots. Widening its repertoire, the city even made a guest appearance in *Indiana Jones and the Last Crusade* (1989), and more recently in Woody Allen's *Everyone Says I Love You* (1997).

Major Festivals

Carnival (Feb/Mar): Lenten jamboree culminating at midnight on Shrove Tuesday.
La Festa di San Marco (25 April): patron saint's day, with gondola race and parade.
La Sensa (Sun after Ascension Day, May): a re-enactment of Venice's Marriage to the Sea when the doge cast a ring into the waves. Today the mayor obliges with a laurel wreath, at San Nicolò on the Lido.
Vogalonga (Sun after La Sensa): colourful regatta from Piazza San Marco to Burano.
Biennale (Jun–Sep): art festival in odd-numbered years.
Festa del Redentore (third Sun in Jul): celebrates deliverance from the 1576 plague with a bridge of boats to Giudecca's Redentore church.
Venice Film Festival (early Sep): a constellation of stars assembles on the Lido.
Regata Storica (first Sun in Sep): a costumed water pageant on the Grand Canal.
Festa della Saluta (21 Nov): Another plague festival with a boat bridge, but to La Salute.

Festivals

Most spectacular of Venice's events is its Lenten **Carnival**, when the city is transformed into an exotic pageant. Masqueraded revellers don weird and wonderful costumes, and everyone has a ball. The carnival dates back over a thousand years, but the wearing of masks became especially fashionable in the 15th century, when party-goers stepped outside the roles dictated by polite society to mingle incognito with other classes. From time to time edicts were issued to curb the wilder excesses, which reached a climax in the late 18th century, when revelry extended for half the year. Napoleon put a stop to this indulgent folly, and the tradition was only revived in 1979, partly as a tourist attraction, since when costumes and masks have assumed ever more elaborate forms. Celebrations end as the chimes of midnight sound on Shrove Tuesday, in a blaze of fireworks over the lagoon.

More solemn are two thanksgiving festivals commemorating Venice's deliverance from the plague. The **Festa del Redentore** in July celebrates the end of an epidemic in 1576, while the **Festa della Salute** on 21 November marks another outbreak in 1630. The two churches that give their names to these festivals were built as memorials to these events. Bridges of boats are formed across the Grand and Giudecca canals, carrying worshippers to Mass. Picnics and fireworks lighten up the proceedings after the services.

Regattas are a typically Venetian way of making merry. Flotillas of beautifully decorated craft sail down the Grand Canal and around the lagoon, while crews in period costume compete in boat races. The most famous events are the **Regata Storica** (historic regatta), held in September, and the feast of **La Sensa** (Sunday after Ascension Day) when the Marriage to the Sea ceremony is re-enacted on the Lido, and a laurel wreath is cast into the waves. The following week, the **Vogalonga** (Long Row) takes place, a 32km (20-mile) race to Burano. Gondoliers, needless to say, play a leading role in these fiercely contested races.

VOGA ALLA VENEZIANA

Rowing in the Venetian manner may look easy, but takes an immense amount of skill. Before they earn a licence, gondoliers undergo years of training (you may spot them practising on Venice's quieter backwaters). The tradition is often handed from father to son. Only one woman (a German) has ever come close to a gondolier's licence (and failed). Gondoliers stand up, facing forwards, one foot ahead of the other, transferring their weight and balance with each stroke. During Venice's regattas and water festivals, racing boats with up to 18 oarsmen can achieve great speed.

On the Waterfront

Just about everything in Venice has to be done by boat, and a short time beside a sizeable canal shows just how busy these watery highways are. A tide of *vaporetti*, water-taxis and motor launches is interspersed by police, fire and ambulance boats, rubbish barges, dredgers, septic-tank emptiers, delivery wherries – even hearses. In the lagoon, cruise liners, naval vessels, cargo boats and oil tankers go to and from the docks of Dorsoduro and Porto Marghera. Once absolutely everything had to be transported to the *centro storico* by boat; now most commodities arrive by air, road or rail, to be discharged before daybreak at Piazzale Roma or Santa Lucia and loaded into a fleet of waiting watercraft and wheeled hand-trolleys for distribution around the city.

Opposite: *Colourful carnival masks fill many a window display in Venice.*
Below: *Waterborne festivals and regattas in period costume make a spectacular sight.*

Venice in Peril

In response to the disastrous floods of 1966, valiant rescue efforts have been made. Some 90 per cent of restoration funds are provided by the Italian government, but about two dozen private organizations in many countries currently work together under UNESCO auspices to restore and conserve Venice's priceless heritage. The stated aim is not to turn the city into a museum or cultural theme park, but to enable it to survive as a living, working city. Funds are allocated, not only for historic monuments, but to modernize ordinary housing stock for Venetian families, in keeping with the city's character. **Venice in Peril Fund**, Morley House, 314–315 Regent Street, London W1R 5AB; tel: 020 7636 6138. **Save Venice Inc.**, 15 East 74th Street, New York 10021, USA; tel: 212 737 3141.

Instantly recognizable is the **gondola**, once the only form of transport, now almost exclusively a pleasure craft. Today there are just a few hundred, where thousands once thronged every canal. They have been made to the same design for centuries in the city's *squeros* (boatyards), of which just a handful remain. For many tourists, a gondola ride is *de rigueur*, but few Venetians ever use them except for weddings or funerals. Most gondoliers have set routes, but for a price are open to negotiation. Besides being expensive, gondola rides can be queasy, smelly and chilly. Not all Venetian rowing boats are gondolas: a bewildering variety includes *sandolos, mascaretas* and *pupparinos* used as fishing, transport and racing vessels.

That Sinking Feeling

Officially, since water extraction from artesian beds was drastically reduced in 1973, Venice has stopped sinking. But sea levels still rise as a result of global warming. Floods were reported as early as AD855. In November 1966, however, water levels rose to 2m (6.5ft) above normal, causing damage compounded by fuel oil spilling from broken storage tanks. These catastrophic floods scarred not only the foundations of buildings, but the city's psyche.

Tidal surges at times fill the lagoon basin to overflowing. It is worse during winter rains and snowmelt, when the Veneto rivers discharge extra volumes. Man-made interventions such as dredging, land reclamation, sea walls and dragnet fishing cause subtle changes to the lagoon currents and increase susceptibility to tidal surges. Today, the area of the *centro storico* affected by winter *acque alte* (high tides) is three times greater than it was a century ago. Freak low tides accompany the surges, beaching boats on mud banks and causing timber foundations to rot on exposure to the air. Even worse for buildings are the continual mini-tides caused by motorized watercraft. These *moto ondoso* (vibrations) cause more damage than temporary inundation.

Below: *Death in Venice – a funeral gondola, painted the traditional dark blue.*

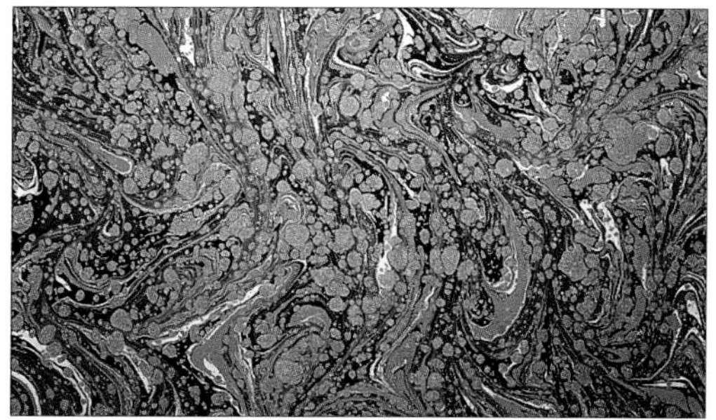

Left: *Marbled paper is one of the city's most distinctive craft specialities.*

Crafts

Glass is so cheap today that it is hard to imagine how highly valued it once was. In earlier centuries, the transformation by fire of humdrum substances like sand and soda into such fragile translucence must have seemed true alchemy. From Roman times, glass-making was a prized skill in the Veneto. When the foundries were relocated to the island of Murano in 1291 to reduce the risk of fire in the city, glass became a prime export commodity. Venice held a European monopoly on mirror-making for centuries. Special techniques produced frosted, enamelled, metallic, filigree or marbled glass, and coloured strands were fused to create cross-sectional *millefiori* patterns. Today, Murano glassware is often regarded as a debased and touristy product, but among much that is mass-produced and clumsy, over-ornate or downright ugly, master craftsmen are still at work on genuinely beautiful and stylish pieces.

Marbled paper is another Venetian speciality, and many lovely shops specialize in this craft around the Frari church, and in Dorsoduro. The technique of marbling originally came from the Far East to Persia and the Arab world. It was brought to Venice by merchant traders, probably in the 13th century. The process of making these unique handblocked patterns using oil-based gums is fascinating and complex. The fan-shaped designs, created with special combs, are more typically Florentine than Venetian.

Mask-making has boomed since the reintroduction of the Carnival in 1979 and the recent explosion of tourism. Garish window displays now grin from street corners.

CRAFT SHOPS

Here is a selection of well-known speciality craft shops.
Glass: **Venini**, fondamenta Vetrai 50, Murano; piazzetta dei Leoncini 314, San Marco. **Seguso**, ponte Vivarini 138, Murano; piazza San Marco 143; Marco Polo Airport. **Barovier e Toso**, fondamenta Vetrai 28, Murano.
Stationery: **Il Pavone**, fondamenta Venier dei Leoni 721, Dorsoduro. **Legatoria Piazzesi**, campiello Feltrina 2551c, San Marco. **Ebru**, campo Santo Stefano 3471, San Marco.
Masks: **Mondonovo**, rio terrà Canal 3063, Dorsoduro. **Ca' Macana**, calle delle Botteghe 3172, Dorsoduro. **Tragicomica**, calle dei Nomboli 2800, San Polo.
Fabrics: **Bevilacqua**, fondamenta Canonica 337b, San Marco. **Norelene**, calle della Chiesa 727, Dorsoduro. **Venetia Studium**, calle Larga XXII Marzo 2403, San Marco; campo dei Frari 3006, San Polo. **Trois**, campo San Maurizio 2666, San Marco.
Lace: **Jesurum**, mercerie del Capitello 4857; piazza San Marco 60/61. **Emilia**, via San Mauro 296–303, Burano. **Dalla Olga**, piazza Galuppi 105, Burano.

Above: *Typical* cichetti *snacks in a bar window.* **Opposite:** *Alfresco dining by the waterfront is one of Venice's eternal pleasures.*

Many are mass-produced, but you can still find hand-decorated masks, traditionally made by a lengthy process using clay, plaster of Paris and papier-mâché. One of the most popular designs is the sinister beaked mask of the Plague Doctor, which was worn during epidemics to protect against infection.

Hand-printed fabrics reflect Venice's trading years of importing silks, damasks, velvets and brocades from the East. Traditional Burano **lace** is hard to find, and very expensive. Today, very few women are willing to wreck their eyesight, and much of what is on sale in local shops and stalls is machined in the Orient. Genuine handmade Burano lace can be found, but at a price, and probably under lock and key in some hidden drawer.

BISCUITS AND BUNS

Sharp-eyed visitors may spot the ancient *forni pubblici* (public bakeries) along Riva degli Schiavoni, not far from the Arsenale. This building once supplied the Venetian armada with ship's biscuit, a staple provision for long sea voyages. Since then the city has diversified and its bakeries are filled with many kinds of biscuits (though some unkindly assert they taste little better). The S-shaped, aniseedy *busolai* are made on Burano; *baicoli* are light, dry dessert biscuits; *zaletti* are made with yellow cornmeal and flavoured with raisins and lemon; *pignoletti* contain pine nuts; *buranelli* resemble shortbread. Carnival treats include calorific *frittelle* (full of cream and raisins) or *crostoli*, flaky pastries dusted with icing sugar.

Food

Venetian cuisine is simple fare – salads and vegetables grown in market gardens (radicchio and asparagus are renowned), and Adriatic seafood. Good cheeses, wines and meats hail from the Veneto, along with wild fungi and game from the mountains. Staples on every menu are rice (grown in the Po Delta) and *polenta*, or maize cornmeal, served boiled, fried or grilled. ***Antipasti*** (hors d'oeuvres) starters generally involve a buffet of tasty bites such as *prosciutto* (Parma ham), *fiori di zucchini* (fried courgette flowers), or *sarde in saor* (sardines in a sweet and sour sauce). The ***primo piatto*** (first course) is often soup, rice or pasta. Typical Venetian specialities include *risi e bisi* (rice and peas), or *pasta e fagioli* (a thick soup with pasta and beans). *Bigoli in salsa* is a local dish of dark spaghetti in an anchovy sauce. *Risotto di mare* is seafood in rice; *spaghetti alle vongole* (with clams) is another classic.

The ***secondo piatto*** stage usually involves fish (these days often frozen and caught some way from the polluted lagoon – it can be expensive, especially if sold by weight) or a meat dish. Vegetables (*contorni*) and salads (*insalata*) are often served as a separate course, and charged extra.

One of the most ubiquitous Venetian dishes is *fegato alla veneziana* (calves' liver and onions, usually served with *polenta*). *Seppie in nero* (squid in its own ink) is another local favourite. *Gambaretti* are prawns (often grilled); *fritto di pesce* or *misto di mare* is a mixed fish grill.

Dolci (desserts) include *tiramisù* (a light but calorific sponge pudding with brandy, coffee and eggs) and ice cream. Coffee is offered with a *digestivo* (liqueur) and perhaps *amaretti* or other biscuit for which Venice is famous.

Harry's Bar

Wreathed in legend, this fashionable watering hole is a quintessential Venetian experience. One story goes that in the early 1930s, barman Giuseppe Cipriani lent cash to a regular American customer, Harry Pickering, who was temporarily down on his luck. To his surprise, Harry came back to repay his debt, plus enough extra to enable Giuseppe to buy up an old ropeworks in Calle Valleresso and set up his own business. Harry's Bar was born: made famous by the likes of Ernest Hemingway, now a place of high prices and international clones. Its celebrated Bellini cocktail (made with white peach juice and Prosecco) is a classic. So too is another speciality named after a Venetian painter – the wafer-thin beef called *carpaccio*. Giuseppe went on to even greater heights with the Cipriani Hotel (now one of the most exclusive in the world). He christened his son and heir Arrigo – the Italian version of Harry.

Cafés and Bars

Cafés are a feature of just about every sizeable Venetian square or waterfront promenade. Most illustrious (and expensive) are the wonderful old coffee houses in Piazza San Marco (Florian, Quadri, etc.), with their rival orchestras. The tempting cakes and pastries are a legacy of the Austrians. Coffee, of course, is an Italian art form, available in a bewildering number of guises from a frothy breakfast *cappuccino* through various milky stages of *latte* and *macchiato* to the mule-kick *espresso doppio* and the secret weapon *corretto* (with a shot of brandy or grappa).

Discover the *cichetti e l'ombra* (a snack with a small glass of wine) and you may never settle for a *menu turistico* again. Try some of Venice's classic ***bacari*** (bars). *Cichetti* are the Italian equivalent of Spanish *tapas*, and involve a mouth-watering array of titbits like spicy meatballs (*polpete*), anchovies (*acciughe*), baby squid (*calamari*), artichoke hearts (*carciofi*), salt cod paste with garlic, parsley and olive oil (*baccala mantecata*), mussels (*cozze*), and a multitude of little triangular sandwiches (*tramezzini*). Some *bacari* provide standing room only; others have tables where you can have a more substantial choice of hot dishes, self-service or brought by a waiter. In some places, it is customary to pay the cashier (*cassa*) in advance for your order and then take the receipt (*scontrino*) to the bar.

2
San Marco

If you fly to Venice's main airport (Marco Polo), take a *vaporetto* or *motoscafo* trip across the lagoon to San Marco. Arriving by water, for centuries the only way to reach the city, is still the most romantic and memorable approach. The *sestiere* of San Marco deserves top billing for many reasons. Geographically, historically and emotionally, this compact district is the heart of Venice. Its main square is one of the western world's most spectacular and distinctive assemblies of art and architecture. Bounded by the breathtaking southerly meander of the Grand Canal, views of and from San Marco's waterfront are some of the most beautiful cityscapes imaginable.

Paradoxically, first impressions of San Marco can take the shine off Venice. Besieged by long queues of tourists for much of the year, its grand set pieces require a lot of time, stamina and concentration to enjoy properly. After a tiring journey, it is easy to notice only the downside of Venice, concentrated in this pressurized part of the city. Here prices are highest, crowds densest, locals tersest, and pigeons everywhere! Conscious of this, Venice's tourist authorities do their best to persuade visitors to disperse and spend time in other areas. San Marco has glamorous shops, fascinating churches, and tranquil neighbourhoods much less thronged than its main square. Let **Piazza San Marco** make its impact gradually. Enjoy a general overview to start with, then rediscover its blockbusting sights in detail after slotting other sections of the city into perspective. Two tourist information centres near the Piazza (*see* page 122) will help you get your bearings.

DON'T MISS

*** **Piazza San Marco:** the biggest and most impressive square in Venice.
*** **Basilica di San Marco:** mosaics, Byzantine treasures and the gilt-bronze horses of the Quadriga.
*** **Doge's Palace:** Venice's seat of government throughout the years of the Republic.
** **Campanile:** city's highest tower with views to the Alps.
** **Museo Correr:** overview of Venetian history, and some wonderful paintings.
** **Campo Santo Stefano:** an attractive square with an exceptional church.

Opposite: *Piazza San Marco, with the Campanile and the Palazzo Ducale.*

Piazza San Marco

Venice's largest square is the only one actually called a piazza (the rest are *campi* or *campielli*). Walled in by theatrical architecture, it has the air of a giant roofless salon in some grand mansion. Napoleon dubbed it Europe's most elegant drawing room. For centuries, Piazza San Marco has been Venice's focal point, once a stage for bullfights, executions, gambling, soliciting, and all kinds of trading. Today, it is a venue for processions, carnivals and street entertainments, a place for strolling, window-shopping, sipping coffee and tuning in to the strains of rival café orchestras. It is one of the lowest-lying areas in the city, and the first to flood at *acqua alta* (high tide) periods, when raised duckboards are placed across its flagstones.

At one end are Venice's two most important monuments, the **Doge's Palace** (the city's earliest citadel and its seat of government for nearly a millennium) and the **Basilica di San Marco**, its most famous church, built to house the relics of its patron saint. Twin Classical columns near the Doge's Palace mark the waterfront approach via a smaller apron-like forum called the **Piazzetta**. West of these are Sansovino's **Zecca**, the city's mint until 1870, and the **Libreria Sansoviniana**, a magnificent library. The rest of the square is surrounded by handsomely matching buildings called the **Procuratie**, originally designed as administrative offices, and now mostly museum space with smart shops and cafés tucked between the arcades. A freestanding bell tower or **Campanile** dominates the centre of the square, and an eyecatching clock tower (**Torre dell'Orologio**) overlooks its northern side.

Dicing with Death

The two granite columns on the Piazzetta came to the city from Tyre in the 12th century. One is topped by a winged lion, symbolizing St Mark, and the other depicts Venice's first patron, St Theodore, dispatching a dragon. Over the centuries, the space between them acquired associations with gambling and public executions. Hanging, beheading and burning at the stake were methods of dispatch, and in 1405 three traitors were buried alive head first. Superstitious Venetians still consider it bad luck to walk between the columns.

Basilica di San Marco ***

This astonishing building is one of the world's most striking churches, a cocktail of eastern and western architectural styles. Its exterior, embellished with arches and columns, spiky finials and bulbous domes, serves merely as an *antipasto* for a dazzling interior of golden mosaics and treasures from Byzantium. The Basilica dates from AD828, when the alleged relics of St Mark the Evangelist arrived in the city from Constantinople, providing Venice with an enormously prestigious patron saint. The present building is the third to stand on this site. The original church burned down in 976, and a second was demolished to make way for an even grander structure in the 11th century, which was adorned with marble and gold and remodelled over many subsequent years. While the Republic lasted, the Basilica functioned as the doge's chapel; only in 1807 did it become the city's cathedral.

Long queues in summer give visitors time to admire the exterior. Mosaics decorate the five large archways of the main façade; the one on the right shows how St Mark's body was stolen from Alexandria by Christian merchants, hidden under a consignment of pork. The large central arch is covered with superb 13th-century carvings depicting a host of subjects, including the signs of the zodiac and the **Labours of the Months**. On the loggia directly above it prance St Mark's famous **bronze horses** (replicas only – the real ones are inside). Crowning the topmost arch is St Mark himself, flanked by angels. On the south face is an exquisite group of porphyry figures known as **The Tetrarchs**, believed to hail from 4th-century Egypt.

Exploring the interior can be frustrating, especially when the city is crowded. Many visitors jostle round San Marco's gloomy one-way system, emerging with a crick in the neck and only the

St Mark's Horses

The bronze horses of San Marco are the only quadriga, or four-horse chariot team, known to have survived from the ancient Classical world, though their precise age and origins are uncertain. After the conquest of Byzantium in 1204, they were taken to Venice from Constantinople's Hippodrome (racecourse). Looted for the second time by Napoleon in 1797, they spent the next few years on the Champs Elysées before returning to San Marco in 1815. Modern copies surmount the cathedral's main entrance; the restored originals stand inside the museum. The distressed surface of the partially gilded bronze is believed to be intentional, heightening the glitter of sunlight and the sense of movement.

Below: *The main façade of the Basilica di San Marco seen from the Piazza.*

Casanova's Escape

Giacomo Casanova made a daring escape from one of the *piombi* cells in the Doge's Palace on Halloween in1755. According to his own, possibly much-embroidered account, his final exit from the prison was aided by a passer-by, who noticed him opening a window. Assuming (because of his fine clothes) that Casanova was some innocent visitor accidentally locked inside the palace, he alerted a guard, who opened the door to the Giants' Staircase. Casanova sauntered coolly past him into the piazza, took a gondola to the mainland and went into exile across the Venetian border. It is said the prison governor received a ten-year sentence for letting him slip the leash.

vaguest notion of its true splendour. Try to time at least one visit when the cathedral is lit up (11:30–12:30 each morning, and during services – Sung Mass at 10:30 on Sundays is unforgettable). Only then can you fully appreciate the rich **mosaics** lining every inch of its walls and five glittering domes, portraying dozens of intricate biblical scenes. The wavering **floors**, equally smothered with geometric and allegorical patterns of marble and glass, also deserve a look.

Separate entrance fees are payable for several of the Basilica's most interesting sights, but these are not exorbitant, and it would be a pity to miss any. The **Treasury** is a spectacular Aladdin's Cave of looted Levantine booty, including chalices and icons of gold and silver, onyx, agate and rock crystal, richly inset with filigree and enamel work. The neighbouring sanctuary houses a macabre array of reliquaries containing gruesome human remains. A spiral staircase near the entrance leads to the **Loggia dei Cavalli** (the outer balcony with the four replica horses which overlooks Piazza San Marco). Don't miss the original horses, protected from pollution and pigeons, which gleam in blue-gold magnificence in an inner room, along with more Medieval treasures. The approach gallery gives you a closer look at the cathedral's ceiling mosaics, and an overview of its Greek Cross plan. Third and perhaps most splendid of these sights is the **Pala d'Oro**, a bejewelled gold-and-silver altar screen behind the high altar. So brilliant is the gem-spangled setting of this 10th-century masterpiece that it all but eclipses the subtle detail of 250 tiny enamel panels embedded within it. One shows the merchant sailors bringing St Mark to Venice on what looks like a sea of blue croquet balls. St Mark's remains are said to lie in a **sarcophagus** beneath the high altar. The canopy (*baldacchino*) above it is supported by carved **alabaster columns**. The Basilica is open 09:45–17:30; museums until 16:00 (except during services). Guided tours in summer.

Below: *The glories of the Basilica di San Marco are its mosaics, only visible when lit up during services.*

Palazzo Ducale ***

Above: *A classic Venetian view of the Doge's Palace, with the twin Classical columns marking the entrance to the Piazzetta.*

Gazing over the Adriatic, which its incumbents dominated for almost a millennium, the Doge's Palace was the engine house of the Venetian Republic, and the most imposing of all its palaces. Its architecture, like that of the adjacent Basilica, is designed to impress. From outside, it looks like an inverted wedding cake. A square block of pink marble rests on a frivolously lacy base of Istrian arcades, as fragile as icing. Inside, there is no doubt about the weighty purpose of this Byzantine Gothic building. The state apartments roll on inexorably, each one grander than its predecessor, with magnificent sculptures and frescoes commissioned from all the formidable artistic talents of the Veneto – Veronese, Bellini, Tintoretto and Titian – for the greater glory of the city-state.

The earliest 'palace' on this site, built in AD814, was really a citadel in which Venice's first rulers took shelter from foreign invasion. Often expanded and restored after fires, it kept its current shape from the early 15th century. More than an official residence, it became the embodiment of La Serenissima's government, where affairs of state were debated, foreign potentates received, legislation approved, and transgressors tried and punished.

From the grand courtyard with its magnificent bronze **wellheads** and carved **capitals** (a café here can provide a welcome shot of caffeine), monumental **staircases** lead to the splendid upper storeys of the palace. Highlights of a lengthy tour are the **Anticollegio** and the **Sala del Maggior Consiglio**, both with Tintoretto masterpieces; the **Sala dello Scudo** or Map Room with globes and charts of Marco Polo's voyages; the **Sala del Consiglio dei Dieci**, where the Council of Ten (an inner cabinet) met to prosecute enemies of the Republic; and the **Sala della Bussola**, where secret denunciations were posted through a *bocca di leone* (lion's mouth). Don't miss Titian's fresco of St Christopher up a hidden stairway, which he dashed

THE MISSING DOGE

The Sala del Maggior Consiglio or grand assembly hall of the Palazzo Ducale contains a frieze of portraits of the first 76 doges of Venice. One space on the Piazzetta wall is occupied by a painted black curtain. This represents the disgraced Doge Marin Falier, beheaded on the steps of the palace for conspiring against the Republic in 1355. Falier gathered together a group of disaffected citizens in an attempt to overthrow the councils and install himself as supreme ruler. It was more common for Venetian doges to be exiled, imprisoned or put to death than to receive any public acclaim for their achievements in office.

For Whom the Bell Tolls

Each of the five bells of the Campanile had a role to play during the days of the Republic. The *marangona* announced the start of the working day; the *nona* rang out at noon. The *mezza terza* summoned senators to the Doge's Palace, and the *trottiera* proclaimed a session of the Great Council. Most doleful of all was the *malefico*, which tolled before an execution. Some unfortunate offenders were imprisoned in a cage and hoisted up the side of the bell tower to dangle for days on end, possibly until they died.

off in just three days, or the psychotic dreamscapes of Hieronymus Bosch in the **Sala dei Tre Capi**. On the first floor lies the impressive **Armoury**, bristling with beautifully crafted ways of death-dealing and a horrifying chastity belt. Even more chilling are the prison cells, where malefactors languished in the dank *pozzi* (wells) near the water line, or sweltered in the *piombi* (leads) under the roof. Leave the palace via the **Porta della Carta**, with its winged lion, which brings you out by the Basilica's south wall. Notice the curious sculpture of San Theodore triumphant on his dragon in the courtyard cloisters; this is the original version of the replica on one of the columns in the Piazzetta. Open daily 09:00–19:00 (17:00 Nov–Mar); last admission 90 min before closing. The audio-guide is recommendable, as are the pricy but enjoyable 'Secret Itinerary' guided tours (in Italian, English or French), which take you round lesser-known sections of this labyrinthine building (tours daily except Wed, 10:30 and 12:00; book ahead on 041 5224951).

Below: *The present Campanile of San Marco dates from the beginning of the 20th century.*

Campanile **

Venice's tallest structure is nearly 100m (323ft) high. This square bell tower of russet brick, topped by a spire with a golden weathervane, has been an unmissable landmark, a watchtower, timekeeper and public address system since the 10th century. It was originally built as a lighthouse to guide sailors on the lagoon. An internal lift gives swift access to the belfry and a panoramic view. Immediately below lie the Basilica's quincunx of domes and the expanse of the piazza. Terracotta roofs stretch towards innumerable water lines. Beyond is the industrialized skyline of Mestre and Marghera, with the Veneto countryside and the Dolomites visible on a clear day. Galileo demonstrated his telescope to the doge from here in 1609. If you happen to be standing beside the five bells as the hour strikes, the din is deafening. The present tower is about a century old; in 1902 its predecessor collapsed in a neat heap in the piazza (miraculously causing little damage to surrounding buildings and harming no-one but an unwary cat which had sidled into the crumbling masonry to finish its breakfast).

Above: *Torre dell'Orologio dominates the north side of the Piazza San Marco.*

Within a decade, an exact replica (*dov'era e com'era* – 'where it was and how it was') had been built, this time with stronger foundations and less weighty brickwork. Sansovino's Classical marble Loggetta was also painstakingly reconstructed at the base of the tower. Open daily 09:00–19:00 (09:30–15:45 in winter).

Torre dell'Orologio **

The ornate clock tower guarding the arched exit from the piazza to the Mercerie was built in the late 15th century. Decorated in blue and gold, the enamelled face displays the phases of the moon and the signs of the zodiac. It was originally built to help sailors plan the most auspicious times for their voyages. On the hour two large dark-bronze figures known as The Moors strike the bell on the roof terrace, and during Ascension week the Magi emerge to pay their respects to the Virgin and Child in the niche above the clock-face. Above this stands yet another of Venice's ubiquitous winged lions. Renovation work by the Geneva watchmaking firm Piaget will keep the clock tower under wraps for some time.

Museums **

Three museums are housed in one complex within the neo-Classical buildings surrounding the piazza, all accessible on a combined ticket with the Doge's Palace. The entrance is in the Ala Napoleonica, or Napoleonic wing, at the end of the square opposite the Basilica. Venice's civic museum is the **Museo Correr**, based on a bequest by the wealthy abbot Teodoro Correr in 1830. It includes works by sculptor Canova, items connected with the history of the Republic (a doge's cap or *zogia*, maps, weaponry, musical instruments, costumes, games), and a fine collection of paintings. Works by Bellini, Vivarini, Mantegna, and many others trace the development of Venetian art from the 14th to 16th centuries. The best-known works are *Two Venetian Ladies* (formerly known as *The Courtesans* – the reputation of these unknown ladies in the low-cut fashions of the

La Vecia del Morter

Near the Torre dell'Orologio is a relief known as *La Vecia del Morter* (the Old Woman of the Mortar). In 1310, **Giustina Rossi** looked from her window over the Sottoportego del Cappello and saw a rebel army passing beneath. This belonged to Bajamonte Tiepolo, a disaffected commander leading a revolt against the doge. By accident or design, Giustina managed to knock Tiepolo's standard-bearer on the head with a stone mortar, which effectively ended the rebellion. As a reward, she had two requests: to hang the Venetian flag from her window on feast days, and to retain the rent on her house at its current rate in perpetuity. Both were granted.

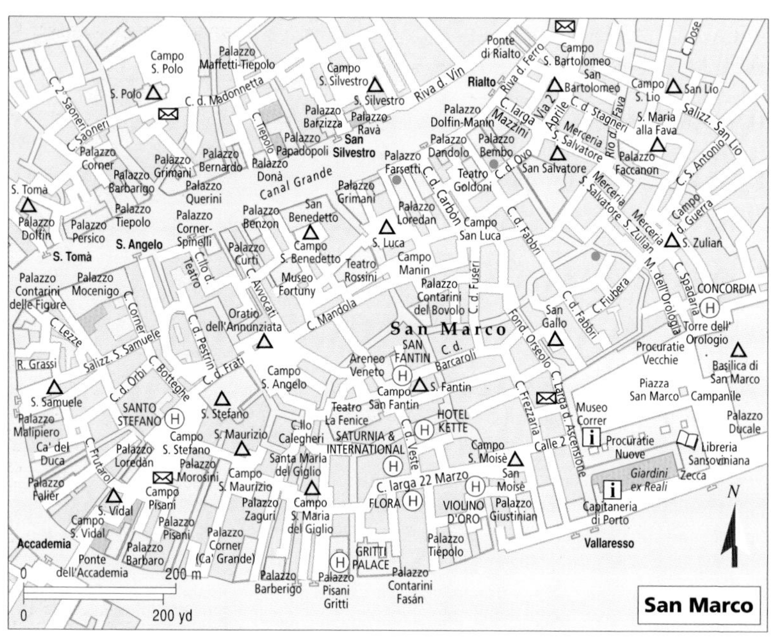

> **Gambling Fever**
>
> Venice's passion for gambling was fuelled by the opening of the **Ridotto** in 1638, in the Palazzo Dandolo off Salizzada San Moisè, where unlucky nobles wiped out fortunes. It closed in 1774, but by 1797 there were 136 gambling dens in rented houses (*casini*). A famous Venetian gambler was Giacomo Casanova, who introduced the lottery to Paris in 1756, then fled to escape creditors. Another was Scottish financier John Law, whose company caused the South Sea Bubble crisis. When shares collapsed he fled to Venice to spend his ill-gotten gains. He is buried in San Moisè church.

early 16th century has recently been salvaged), and *A Portrait of a Young Man in a Red Hat*, both by Carpaccio.

The **Museo Archeologico** displays Greek and Roman sculpture, mostly assembled by Doge Antonio Grimani's son Domenico, and bequeathed to the state in 1523.

The **Libreria Sansoviniana** has a valuable assortment of rare early maps and illuminated manuscripts in two lavishly painted halls. Sansovino's Classical building was extravagantly praised by the great Renaissance architect Andrea Palladio, though frost damage caused the ceiling to collapse during its construction. Open daily, Nov–Mar 09:00–17:00; Apr–Oct 09:00–19:00.

West of the Piazza

Yellow signs indicate the way to the Accademia from the west end of the piazza. Through the arcades by the APT tourist office, streets are filled with elegant shops, many sporting big names like Bruno Magli, Versace, Kenzo and Armani. African street traders hawk Vuitton look-alikes from pavement pitches outside. Calle Vallaresso leads to a waterfront landing stage and the legendary **Harry's Bar** (*see* page 29), where visitors look for Hemingway's ghost among expensive Bellini cocktails. Famously hideous, the exuberant Baroque façade of **San Moisè** has a bizarre gusto (spot the comical camel). Further west, the chapels of **Santa Maria del Giglio** (also known as Santa Maria Zobenigo) contain a Tintoretto (*The Evangelists*, over the high altar) and a putative Rubens in the sacristy. Its façade commemorates the Barbaro family, who financed it. A block or so north lies the site of the unhappy **Teatro La Fenice**, struggling through engineering problems and financial doldrums to rise once more from its ashes. The nearby **San Fantin** church has a lovely apse by Sansovino. Campo San Maurizio is a venue for antiques fairs and exhibitions.

RISING FROM THE ASHES

The word *fenice* means 'phoenix' in Italian, an apt name for a notoriously flammable theatre. The original Fenice burnt down in 1836, but was replaced within a year. On 29 January 1996, it was destroyed by fire again, this time deliberately, by construction workmen anxious to avoid penalties for failing to meet repair deadlines. Two electricians were imprisoned for arson a year later. But this time the poor phoenix seems mired in a morass of technical and financial problems. The recent discovery of important archaeological finds on the site looks set to delay its reconstruction still further. In the meantime, the Fenice opera company stages performances in a marquee called the Palafenice, on the 'car-park' island of Tronchetto west of Piazzale Roma.

Santo Stefano **

This delightful church is easily spotted by the alarming list of its tower. Dating from the 14th century, it has a carved doorway by Bartolomeo Bon. Inside, its principal glory is its fine ship's-keel roof, braced by decorated tie-beams and marble pillars. Light floods into the upper nave from lunette windows, giving it a calmness which belies its violent history – it was deconsecrated half a dozen times because of the mayhem that regularly broke out within its walls. Two well-known Venetians are buried here: the composer Gabrieli and Doge Francesco Morosini, whose Peloponnese campaigns caused horrific damage to the Parthenon. Several works of art can be seen in the sacristy, including late paintings by Tintoretto. Open Mon–Sat 10:00–17:00; Sun 13:00–17:00. Member of Chorus scheme (*see* page 20), entrance fee for sacristy. The *campo* bearing the same name is one of Venice's largest squares, a popular café scene surrounded by fine palazzi. The renowned *gelateria* Paolin provides an excuse to stop and admire them for a while over a pistachio ice cream.

Below: *The leaning tower of Santo Stefano church, seen from neighbouring Campo San Maurizio.*

Mariano Fortuny

Born in Catalonia, Fortuny was something of a polymath, showing talent in several scientific and creative fields: physics, chemistry, painting, photography, architecture, engraving, sculpture, and theatrical design. His name lives on, however, in the world of *haute couture*, where his pleated silk dresses became all the rage during the 1920s. The early process of pleating, patented in 1909, was agonizing – each separate fold had to be positioned by hand in wet material, sewn in place, and fixed with a hot iron. The result was a garment so fine it could be threaded through a wedding ring.

Museo Fortuny *

Spanish designer Mariano Fortuny y Madrazo moved to Venice in 1889, spending much of his life in the splendid Gothic Palazzo Pesaro, which hosts occasional exhibitions revealing his multifaceted interests. He is best remembered for his slinky pleated fabrics created by traditional Renaissance methods using ancient dyes. Fortuny textiles are still on sale in Venice, sometimes made into lampshades. Peep into the courtyard if you're passing.

Palazzo Contarini del Bovolo *

Signposted through labyrinthine alleys from Campo Manin, this building's most striking feature is its 'snailshell' (*bovolo*) external staircase, a 15th-century helter-skelter of elegant loggias and arches. For a small fee you can climb to the top of the tower. Open daily, Apr–Oct 10:00–18:00.

Heading for the Rialto

The Torre dell'Orologio on the northern side of the piazza points the way to the Rialto via a narrow thoroughfare known as the **Mercerie**. Constantly awash with a tide of tourists, this chain of streets is mostly devoted to shopping, as its name suggests. Nowadays, the exotic-sounding brocades, silks, spices and caged nightingales described by travellers in earlier centuries have been largely replaced by Murano glass trinkets, mass-produced carnival masks, high-street fashion and fast-food restaurants. If you find it too commercialized, the parallel Calle del Fabbri makes a quieter alternative. Following the Mercerie, however, brings you along a route past the following sights.

Opposite: *The flamboyant staircase of the Palazzo Contarini del Bovolo.*
Below: *Gondolas glide past the ornate façade of San Moisè church.*

San Zulian *

Venetian dialect turns San Giuliano (this church's official name) into 'Zulian'. A refit by Sansovino in 1553 shaped its present appearance in white Istrian stone, but it is San Zulian's wealthy benefactor who is remembered above the entrance door. The scholarly physician Tommaso Rangone

is immortalized in bronze with his books and globes. The square, spacious interior is richly endowed with sombre ceiling frescos by Palma il Giovane, as well as gilded woodwork and sculpture by Campagna. Open Mon–Sat 08:30–12:00, Sun 17:00–20:00.

San Salvatore **

This fine 16th-century Renaissance church reveals the hand of several important artists, notably Tullio Lombardo and Sansovino. The grey-white interior of chilly geometric spaces, lightened by lantern domes, contains some interesting monuments. One is the Mannerist tomb of Doge Francesco Venier, another a memorial to Caterina Cornaro, whose arranged marriage and widowhood (by poisoning) added Cyprus to La Serenissima's many ill-gotten gains. Two paintings by Titian – a *Transfiguration* altarpiece (1560) with Christ's robes billowing amid the outstretched limbs of awestruck disciples, and *The Annunciation* (third altar on the right), plus Bellini's *Supper at Emmaus* are other artistic highlights. Open daily 09:00–12:00, 16:00–19:00.

Campo San Bartolomeo *

The statue of playwright Carlo Goldoni (1707–93) smiles indulgently at the young revellers who gather in this bustling square near the Rialto, a popular meeting place at *passegiata* time, when the cafés and bars, including its branch of McDonald's, hum with life. At one end of the square the minor church of San Bartolomeo, stripped of treasures which once included a Dürer altarpiece (now in Prague), provides space for the odd exhibition. A sizeable community of German merchants once occupied this area: the Fondaco dei Tedeschi at the north end of the square, whose handsome façade makes a fine landmark on the Grand Canal, was used as a warehouse and social centre. It is now Venice's main post office.

Caterina Cornaro

This unhappy lady, daughter of a noble Venetian family, was betrothed at only 14 to the King of Cyprus. Soon after this loveless match, the king died in suspicious circumstances (allegedly poisoned on Doge Venier's orders). Caterina became a helpless pawn in a political chess game between Venice, Turkey and a wicked mother-in-law, who probably murdered Caterina's infant son. With enemies on all sides, Caterina ceded Cyprus to La Serenissima and abdicated to lead a quiet life in Asolo. Venetian spies kept her under surveillance, bumping off real or imagined lovers to avoid prospective heirs with dynastic ambitions. If it made her life a misery, at least Venice gave her a decent funeral. She is buried in a fine tomb in San Salvatore church under her former title, Queen of Cyprus.

DANIELI

3 Castello

Castello is Venice's largest, leafiest *sestiere*, stretching east of the Doge's Palace along the popular Riva degli Schiavoni to the quiet sectors of Sant'Elena and San Pietro. A stroll through eastern Castello's streets, stacked with colourful market stalls and billowing with drying laundry, is the perfect antidote to an overdose of Tiepolo. Castello is a rare part of Venice containing a significant amount of unbuilt land. Besides providing green breathing space, the Giardini Pubblici (public gardens) offer a forum for one of the major cultural events, the Biennale.

On a map, Castello's most striking feature is obvious. The huge shipyards of the Arsenale once resounded with the hammering of thousands of workers engaged in La Serenissima's formidable war machine. Today, these colossal docks lie silent, inaccessible to all but a handful of naval personnel. Sadly, the *vaporetto* route which once gave visitors a tantalizing glimpse of this extraordinary piece of industrial heritage has been discontinued.

East of the Arsenale is the island of San Pietro, site of the vanished 8th-century fortress (*castello*) which gave this district its name, and Venice's neglected former cathedral. Before it was superseded by San Marco in the early 19th century, San Pietro was the official headquarters of Venetian religious life.

Most visitors stick to the areas west of the Arsenale, which contain a number of important churches, several worthwhile museums, and long stretches of quayside with sweeping water views. Riva degli Schiavoni is the main springboard for the southern islands of the lagoon.

Don't Miss

*** **Riva degli Schiavoni:** glorious waterfront views, history and architecture, including the Bridge of Sighs.
*** **Santi Giovanni e Paolo:** largest, most important church after Basilica di San Marco.
** **Museo Storico Navale:** Venice's maritime history from triremes to torpedoes.
** **Scuola di San Giorgio degli Schiavoni:** Carpaccio's unforgettable paintings.
** **San Zaccaria:** Gothic and Renaissance masterpieces.
** **Campo Santa Maria Formosa:** fine architecture and art in the church.

Opposite: *The Danieli Hotel – an imposing sight on the Riva degli Schiavoni.*

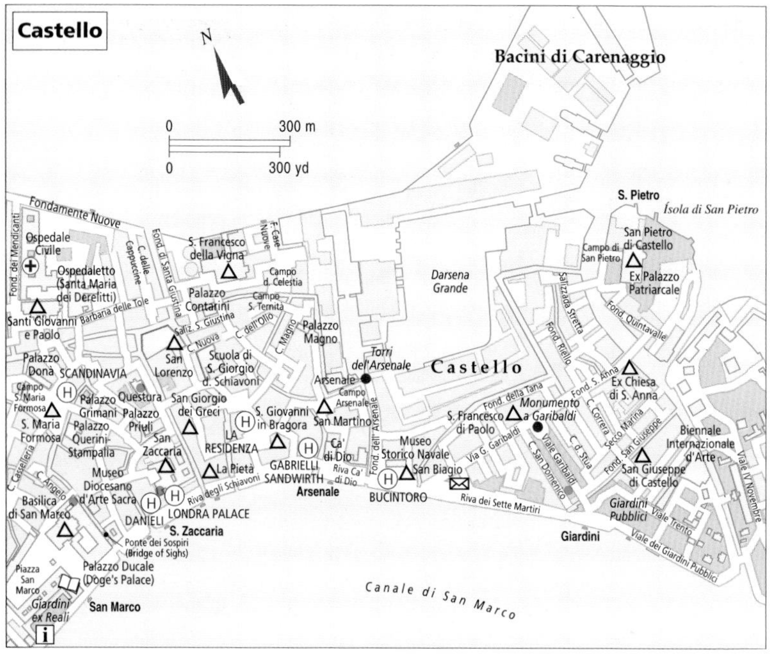

Riva degli Schiavoni

Tides of tourists spill along this broad, paved esplanade to enjoy the superb panorama of San Giorgio Maggiore, and capture that mandatory snapshot of the **Bridge of Sighs** from the Ponte della Paglia. The name of the street originates from Dalmatian or Slavic traders (Schiavoni) who frequented the area in Medieval times, when it must have been a chaotic jostle of galleons and merchandise from all over the known world. The quayside is just as busy these days, though the cargoes are mostly human. The amorphous welter of global sightseers is punctuated by identifiable groups: nuns, sailors on shore leave, *carabinieri*, street traders and gondoliers with their wheedling cries. Gondolas seesaw in the wake left by darting *vaporetti*, water-taxis, and excursion boats. Occasional liners or naval vessels lend a more stately tone to the scene. Terrace restaurants and café-bars, souvenir shops, travel agencies

Coffee

The Venetians were the first to introduce the Italians to this strange black drug, which the doge's ambassador to Constantinople reported seeing the Turks drink during the 1580s. Coffee eventually reached Italy in 1640, and was originally regarded as a medicine: 'They say it has the ability to keep people awake'. The caffeine habit caught on, and Venice's first coffee house opened in 1683, on the site occupied by Caffè Florian since 1720. At one time there were over 20 similar cafés in the arcades of the Piazza San Marco alone.

and hotels occupy this desirable stretch of waterfront; even modest guesthouses can command high prices for the views. The **Hotel Danieli** is one of the most prominent landmarks. This eyecatching Gothic building, originally the 14th-century Palazzo Dandolo, has seen many famous literary and artistic guests. Petrarch found inspiration for his courtly love poems at a house nearby, and Henry James completed *The Portrait of a Lady* at No. 4161.

Production Liners

The *arsenalotti* were one of the first workforces in Europe to use sophisticated assembly-line methods of production, foreshadowing the Industrial Revolution. At top speed, at least one ship a day could be made ready for the fleet. The completed vessels were equipped with arms and supplies as they were towed past warehouses and by the time they reached the open water, they were fit for action. During a visit by Henry III of France in 1574, a warship was constructed in the time it took the king to eat a banquet. No doubt this dissuaded him from any plans to challenge Venice's maritime supremacy.

Ponte dei Sospiri **

The Bridge of Sighs is one of Venice's most famous landmarks, a stock image of the postcard trade. If you have visited the Doge's Palace you may well have walked across this covered bridge of white Istrian stone. Built in 1600, it linked the law courts with the new prisons across the water in Castello. Through the ornamental window grills, condemned wretches caught their last glimpses of the sunlit lagoon ... or so the legend popularized by 19th-century Romantic writers goes. By the standards of their time, the new prisons weren't too ghastly. Casanova had decent food and clean laundry. His gaoler was mystified by his reluctance to be moved to a better cell with fresh air and a good view, but the reason soon became clear – he was just completing an escape tunnel from his old quarters.

Below: *The much photographed Bridge of Sighs.*

La Pietà *

The Classical exterior of this small church is easily spotted along the Riva degli Schiavoni. Surprisingly, the façade dates only from 1906, although the original building, remodelled in the mid-18th century, dates back to the 1600s. Often known as 'Vivaldi's church', its prettily frescoed, oval interior can be seen only during the concerts

regularly held to commemorate the work of the great composer who was choirmaster at La Pietà for nearly 40 years (*see* panel, page 23). The ceiling was painted by Giambattista Tiepolo. The church's décor and excellent acoustics go some way towards compensating for its unforgiving pews, which prevent visitors dozing off through yet another rendition of *The Four Seasons*.

Museo Storico Navale **

If you have the least interest in Venice's maritime history, don't miss this museum near the Arsenale *vaporetto* station. An extensive collection of exhibits includes naval weaponry, historic photographs, charts, models, figureheads, navigational instruments and globes. The ground floor is devoted to sea warfare, with cannon, chained projectiles designed to foul the masts of enemy ships, and manned torpedoes used in World War II. Highlights on the upper floors range from a magnificent scale replica of the doge's ceremonial barge (the *Bucintoro*) to a model of a typical oar-driven trireme (galley) used in the Venetian fleet. Head to the third floor for a close-up of some splendid gondolas, including one once privately owned by Peggy Guggenheim. Chinese junks recall the voyages of Marco Polo, while the top floor contains an impressive collection of shells. Labelling is in English as well as Italian. Open Mon–Sat 08:45–13:30.

Below: *The church of La Pietà, a popular venue for Vivaldi concerts, on the Riva degli Schiavoni.*

Arsenale **

The dockyards are currently under naval administration and inaccessible to the general public, though plans are afoot to make more use of this fascinating area. The crenellated monumental gateway with its strange lions and twin towers gives some idea of its grandeur. It dates from 1460, and is one of the city's earliest Renaissance buildings. During its 16th-century heyday, the Arsenale was a hive of activity. Some 16,000 highly organized workers beavered away to construct and repair the Venetian fleet. Dante is said to have marvelled at the frenzied goings-on in the Arsenale, and transformed the caulking vats of boiling tar he had seen into one of the torments of the *Inferno*. An old rope factory nearby is used for Biennale exhibition space.

Above: *Venice's Naval Museum occupies an old warehouse near the Arsenale dockyards.*

Eastern Castello

Few tourists find time or inclination to stray beyond the Naval Museum. Yet a stroll through the working-class residential quarters of eastern Castello, though scarcely essential viewing, gives a welcome flavour of everyday community life often lacking in rarefied central Venice. The main choice of routes is to follow the waterfront through the **Giardini Pubblici**, or to head inland along the **Viale Garibaldi**, a broad, busy street which Napoleon created by filling in a canal. Here locals walk their dogs, meet to chat in small bars or family *trattorie*, and shop for groceries and cakes at the street market. Stalls are piled high with glistening eels, artichokes in oil, and unidentifiable autumn fungi. John and Sebastian Cabot, discoverers of Newfoundland, lived in the first house on the right. At the far southeast end of Castello is the area known as **Sant'Elena**, until recently undeveloped meadowland surrounded by the open lagoon. During the Austrian occupation, troops used it for exercise and training. Today it contains the city's football stadium, a naval college and a small Gothic church dedicated to St Helena (the mother of Constantine) with a fine door carving. Further north, the cathedral island of **San Pietro** is anchored to central Venice by a couple of spindly bridges. To the west, washing decks the grid-like courts of Sant'Anna's 19th-century houses like festive bunting.

Santa Barbara

Palma il Vecchio's polyptych featuring *St Barbara and Saints* (1510) in the church of Santa Maria Formosa is a masterpiece. Its central panel depicts the saint calmly facing her martyrdom at the hands of her father, who was promptly struck by lightning. St Barbara thus became associated with sudden death in thunderstorms or by artillery fire (note the cannon-balls in the chapel). The Confraternity of Bombardiers commissioned this picture of their patron saint. George Eliot described this striking painting as 'an almost unique presentation of a hero-woman'. The model is alleged to have been the artist's daughter.

Giardini Pubblici *

As urban parks go, these public gardens are no great shakes, but the shady gravelled walkways offer enticing waterfront views (glorious at sunset) with benches to sit and listen to birdsong. Cats hunt in the undergrowth, while children play on the swings. Monumental statuary adds a few focal points. Garibaldi strikes a heroic pose astride a rocky mini-mountain in the tree-lined avenue which bears his name; Minerva rides a dopey-looking lion side-saddle; the half-submerged bronze on the Riva dei Sette Martiri commemorates the women who were killed in World War II. The main interest of the gardens is the international pavilions which host the Biennale exhibition of avant-garde contemporary art every alternate summer.

Best Viewpoints

A few spots in Venice offer unrivalled vistas of the city.

- **Loggia dei Cavalli:** the bronze horses of San Marco have a view of the piazza.
- **Campanile:** views of the Alps on a clear day.
- **Hotel Danieli:** the roof terrace has an expensive but panoramic restaurant.
- **Ca' d'Oro:** fine views of the Grand Canal from the loggia.
- **Ponte di Rialto:** a bustling watercraft scene.
- **Ponte dell'Accademia:** palaces, gondolas and the church of La Salute.
- **Punta della Dogana:** view of St Mark's Basin and the mouth of the Grand Canal.
- **Zattere** and **Riva degli Schiavoni:** promenades overlooking the Giudecca and San Giorgio Maggiore.
- **San Giorgio Maggiore:** possibly the best view of all, of the lagoon and the city.

San Pietro di Castello *

A drunkenly tilted campanile dominates the small island of San Pietro, one of Venice's earliest settlements, whose church, founded here in the 7th century, became the city's cathedral from 1451 until 1807. Its location, far removed from San Marco, ensured there was no undue meddling by the Vatican in the Republic's affairs. It stands in a grassy, rather run-down square. The present building dates from the mid-16th century, in a ponderous Palladian style. The massive cupola was added in 1670. Inside, the glass coffin of San Lorenzo Giustiniani, first Patriarch of Venice, is borne aloft by angels and *putti* (cherubs) on an elaborate altarpiece of white marble. The 13th-century so-called 'Throne of St Peter', a marble seat made from an Arabic funeral stone, stands in the right aisle. Open Mon–Sat 10:00–17:00; Sun 13:00–17:00. Member of Chorus scheme (*see* page 20).

Northwest Castello

West of the Arsenale, the narrow, maze-like streets of Castello are packed with sights, many of them churches. Everyone's list includes the huge **Santi Giovanni e Paolo**, one of Venice's most important religious buildings, and **San Zaccaria**, full of artistic treasures. But

Castello's less well-known churches are just as rewarding. Gaunt **San Francesco della Vigna**, imposing **Santa Maria Formosa**, modest **San Giovanni in Bragora**, iconic **San Giorgio dei Greci** – all have their charms. The great variety of these churches avoids tedium, though seeing too many in a day may well induce cultural overload. Two fine *scuole* and several interesting museums provide a change of scene, along with countless crumbling palazzi on atmospheric squares. Some, at least, are adequately provisioned with cafés and ice-cream shops. Otherwise, make a beeline for the waterfront and recharge your batteries with a ride round the lagoon.

Bartolomeo Colleoni

Outside San Zanipolo stands one of Venice's most famous equestrian monuments, commemorating Bartolomeo Colleoni, a great military hero of Renaissance times. The story goes that Colleoni left his estate to the Republic on condition that a statue be erected in his memory in St Mark's Square. The cynical city fathers agreed, took the money, then reneged on the deal, salving their consciences by putting him outside the Scuola di San Marco instead. In retrospect, Colleoni may not be too unhappy; this is a fine setting, with fewer pigeons.

San Francesco della Vigna **

The 'vineyard' (*vigna*) in this rather remote part of northern Castello was part of an estate donated to the Franciscan community in 1253. The monks built a church here soon afterwards, which was fashionably expanded by Sansovino and Palladio in the 16th century. Initial impressions of the grey, barrel-vaulted nave with multiple side-chapels are a bit dispiriting, but its treasures encompass charming bas-relief carvings by Pietro Lombardo in the Cappella Giustiniani (to the left of the chancel) and a *Madonna and Saints* by Bellini in the Cappella Santa. Save some coins to light up Antonio da Negroponte's gorgeous *Madonna and Child Enthroned* in the right transept, exquisitely detailed with flowers and birds. The familiar robed figure of St Francis presides over the tranquil cloisters of cypress and oleander, and on one of the stoups near the west door in an inspired miniature bronze by Alessandro Vittoria. Open daily 08:00–12:30, 15:00–19:00.

Below: *Bartolomeo Colleoni's heroic equestrian statue graces the square near the massive church of Santi Giovanni e Paolo.*

Santi Giovanni e Paolo ***

Venetians call this basilica San Zanipolo, and it ranks (with St Mark's and the Frari) as one of Venice's most significant sacred buildings. Built by Dominican friars in the 13th and 14th centuries, its inner dimensions are instantly impressive, with an

apse flooded by light from double-tiered lancets. Wooden tie beams detract slightly from the austere lines of the soaring nave. The interior of rosy brick and Istrian stone is stuffed with monuments – 25 doges are buried here. Lombardo's tombs for Pietro Mocenigo (1481), Nicolò Marcello (1474), and Andrea Vendramin (1476–78) are some of his greatest masterpieces. Works by Paolo Veronese decorate the Rosary Chapel; a Bellini altarpiece illuminates the right aisle; stained glass from Murano glows in the right transept.

The *campo* on which this massive church stands is one of the largest and most handsome in Venice. Outside San Zanipolo is the contrasting façade of the 15th-century **Scuola di San Marco** in white marble, decorated with a wonderful series of trompe l'œil panels. At present it houses the city hospital. You can peer inside the reception foyer, but you need special permission to see the chapel or the library. Just off the square is the Ospedaletto, or Santa Maria dei Derelitti, a charitable institution in which orphaned girls studied music. The façade is carved with grotesques; inside are prettier frescoes by Tiepolo. Open Mon–Sat 10:00–17:00, Sun 13:00–17:00.

Below: *The church of Santi Giovanni e Paolo, known to Venetians as San Zanipolo, makes a grand statement in northwest Castello.*

Campo Santa Maria Formosa **

This large market square was once the scene of bullfights and other forms of entertainment; today it is still a lively place with a number of antique stalls and cafés. The Palazzo Priuli is just one of several elegant buildings surrounding it. Pride of place, however, goes to the large and aptly named church which dominates the *campo* (the word *formosa* means buxom or handsome), one side facing the square, another the nearby canal. Curvaceous apses, a cupola and a Baroque façade grace the main building; next to it is a late 17th-century campanile with a grotesque face. Inside, the Greek Cross structure is memorable, and the walls are decked with real treasures, including a Byzantine icon, a Vivarini triptych, and a superb multi-panelled work by Palma il Vecchio, featuring St Barbara in flowing red robes, surrounded by saints. Open Mon–Sat 10:00–17:00, Sun 13:00–17:00. Member of Chorus scheme (*see* page 20).

Above: *Santa Maria Formosa's fine campanile was added in 1688.*

Palazzo Querini-Stampalia *

This lovely 16th-century palazzo, together with its contents, was bequeathed to Venice through a charitable organization by the last of the wealthy and influential Querini family in 1868. Imaginatively restored, it offers visitors a chance to peep inside an authentic Renaissance home, mostly furnished in 18th-century style. Streamlined modern exhibition space designed by Carlo Scarpa provides a foil for displaying porcelain, furniture and an interesting if rather uneven collection of paintings (including a Bellini or two). Upstairs is a well-used reference library. The best way to enjoy this building is to catch one of its evening concerts held amid the Murano chandeliers and frilly plasterwork on the first floor (concerts are included in the admission price). The gallery is open Tue–Thu and Sun, 10:00–13:00 and 15:00–18:00; Fri–Sat until 22:00.

Museo Diocesano d'Arte Sacra*

The Benedictine monastery of Sant'Appollonia makes an attractive setting for a collection of sacred art, not far from the Bridge of Sighs. If it gives the impression of being something of a holy jumble sale, this is because much of its content changes regularly. The museum provides a refuge for treasures in need of restoration from damaged or deconsecrated churches, and also acts as a temporary clearing house for stolen items retrieved by Italy's vigilant art police. Its beautifully restored Romanesque cloister makes a good reason to visit. Open Mon–Sat 10:30–12:30. There is no formal admission charge, though a donation is requested.

MATCHMAKING

San Pietro is associated with mass wedding ceremonies. During the 10th century, a band of Slav pirates burst into the church and abducted several brides, together with their dowries. The Venetians gave chase and rescued the women, who were reunited with their rightful husbands. Every year, this incident was commemorated in the **Festival of the Marys**, when two girls were chosen from each *sestiere* and married in a single ceremony at the cathedral, followed by eight days of feasting and fun.

Above: *Gondolier-style straw boaters make a popular souvenir.*

San Zaccaria **

Built on ancient foundations now below the water table, San Zaccaria's façade combines Gothic and Classical Renaissance styles with great success. Inside, amid a welter of sombre ecclesiastical art, Giovanni Bellini's masterpiece *Madonna and Child with Saints* (1505) glows in jaw-dropping splendour in the north aisle. Relics of the church's patron, San Zaccaria (father of John the Baptist), lie on the opposite side. Entrance charges are made for two inner chapels off the right nave, but these are not to be missed. Sant'Athanasio contains intricate choir stalls and fine if unhappily lit works by Tintoretto and Tiepolo; San Tarasio beyond contains magnificent Gothic altarpieces by Vivarini and Alemagna in rich gold settings. Frescoes by Andrea del Castagno adorn the walls. The mosaic floors heave with subsidence, and an eerie silent pond in the vaulted crypt drowns the last resting place of eight doges. Open daily 10:00–12:00, 16:00–18:00. Member of Chorus scheme (*see* page 20).

Naughty Nuns

The Benedictine convent next to San Zaccaria is now a police station for Venice's gun-toting *carabinieri*. The high-spirited nuns who preceded them were anything but law-abiding. Many had no particular spiritual vocation, but were young girls from high-born Venetian families locked up here for wilful behaviour or to avoid the expense of a marriage dowry. Tales of masked balls, amorous liaisons and wild parties circulated during the 18th century, and the nuns' parlour became a fashionable salon. When officials arrived to investigate these rumours, they were pelted with bricks.

San Giorgio dei Greci *

A typical leaning campanile marks the site of this quiet enclave belonging to Venice's Greek community, who made a scholarly contribution in Renaissance times. Reached along a gated canalside path, its Classical weatherstained exterior seems quite unexceptional. The Orthodox interior, however, contains a startlingly gorgeous iconostasis (altar screen), smothered in gilded icons of haloed saints and angels, which completely covers the east wall, concealing the high altar. The nave is flanked by dark choir stalls and surmounted by a lantern dome. Above the main entrance is a raised gallery where the women sit apart, as in a synagogue. The building next to the church is the Hellenistic Institute's **Museo di Dipinti Sacri Bizantini**, containing a collection of jewel-coloured 14th- to 18th-century icons. Open Mon–Sat 09:00–12:30 and 13:30–16.30; Sun 10:00–17:00.

Scuola di San Giorgio degli Schiavoni **

Established in 1451 by Dalamatian merchants and fishermen, the glory of this simple confraternity building is an astonishing cycle of paintings by Vittore Carpaccio. Nine huge linen canvases deck the ground-floor chamber, three each devoted to St George, St Tryphon and St Jerome. Most mesmerizing is the first in the series, in which St George plunges his lance into the jaws of a fearsome frill-winged dragon. A tranquil backdrop of Renaissance buildings and landscape contrasts gruesomely with the scattered limbs and bones of the creature's hapless victims in the foreground. The upper room with its painted timbers and portraits honouring the worthy patrons of the *scuola* is inevitably an anticlimax after this *tour de force*. Open Tue–Sat 09:00–12:30 and 15:30–18:30; Sun 09:30–12:30.

San Giovanni in Bragora *

This deceptively simple late Gothic structure houses a luminous collection of art. Beneath an original ship's-keel ceiling, works by the Vivarini family (*Madonna Enthroned with Saints*; *Resurrection*) and Cima de Conegliano (*Baptism of Christ*) are the main points of interest. Note the font in which Vivaldi was christened, left of the main entrance. He spent much of his early life on the Campo Bandiera e Moro outside, on which stand some fine old palaces. Most striking is the 15th-century Palazzo Gritti Badoer, now renovated as La Residenza hotel (*see* Where to Stay, page 116). Open Mon–Sat 09:00–11:00, Mon–Fri 17:00–19:00.

Baffling the Postman

Venetian postal addresses defy practical logic. Within each *sestiere*, every building is given a separate number, but the street name is generally missing, e.g. San Marco 2917. Make sure, before you set off for any destination, that you know the street or square, or a nearby landmark. The usual word for street is *calle*, but here are some others:

- ***fondamenta:*** a quayside street running alongside a canal, often named after it
- ***riva:*** a quay or promenade, often facing the open lagoon
- ***rio terra:*** a filled-in canal
- ***piscina:*** a filled-in square
- ***sotoportico/sotoportego:*** a covered arcade cutting through a terrace of buildings
- ***salizzada:*** a main through route
- ***ruga:*** main shopping street
- ***corte:*** literally a courtyard, but often just a narrow alley between houses
- ***ramo:*** a short cul-de-sac
- ***campo:*** square (San Marco is Venice's only piazza)
- ***campiello:*** tiny square.

Left: *Yellow street signs guide visitors through Venice's maze of alleys.*

4
Cannaregio

Cannaregio arcs round the northern reaches of the Grand Canal between the Rialto and the Ponte dei Scalzi. Broad canals and vistas of the open lagoon give this second-largest *sestiere* an even more aqueous feel than usual in Venice. During the Middle Ages this part of the city was extremely marshy and malarial; the canals acted as drainage ditches when the reed swamps were cleared. Long paved quays (*fondamente*) line many of its internal waterways. Cannaregio is now mainly residential – home to over a third of the city's permanent inhabitants. Two of Venice's most important artists, **Titian** and **Tintoretto**, spent most of their lives here, and **Marco Polo** began his fabulous voyages from somewhere near the Rialto.

Most of the best sights lie towards its eastern end; the west is a fairly drab area dominated by Venice's central railway station. Yet a mere stone's throw away lie quiet, virtually unvisited working districts of village-like charm, where cats wait beady eyed for fishy scraps trawled from the canals, and tiny corner shops stock hardware and washing powder instead of keepsakes for tourists.

Like all Venice's *sestieri*, Cannaregio is stuffed with churches. At opposite ends of some spectrum or other lie the extraordinary Baroque church of the **Gesuiti** with its fluid cladding of sea-green marble damask, and the crisply starched Gothic niches of **Madonna dell'Orto**. No-one should miss the bandbox perfection of **Santa Maria dei Miracoli**, or the candlelit intimacy of **San Giovanni Crisostomo**. Even churches declared 'of no interest' by some authorities repay a glance with an architectural

Don't Miss

*** **Ca' d'Oro:** the best of the Grand Canal's palatial façades, and a fine collection of *objets d'art*.
*** **Santa Maria dei Miracoli:** inlaid marble, serpentine and jasper.
*** **Madonna dell'Orto:** Tintoretto's church – delightful inside and out.
** **Gesuiti:** chilly but impressive church with astonishing trompe l'œil marble interior.
** **The Ghetto:** Venice's atmospheric Jewish quarter.
** **Campo dei Mori:** turbaned merchants on a picturesque canalside square.

Opposite: *Santa Maria dei Miracoli, one of Venice's best-loved churches.*

The statue near the church of Santa Fosca along the Strada Nova is dedicated to a high-minded and intellectual priest who dared to challenge the authority of Rome. Sarpi was a renowned historian, an amateur scientist and a friend of Galileo. A highly respected adviser to the doge, he was implicated in events leading to the Great Interdict of 1606, in which the entire city of Venice was ex-communicated. Afterwards he was savagely attacked at Santa Fosca by a posse of assassins (presumably commissioned by the Vatican) who plunged a stiletto blade into his face and left him for dead. Amazingly, he survived the ordeal to enjoy a handsome state pension for a further 22 years.

surprise or vignette of Venetian life. Mothers gather for a harmless teatime gossip in the tiny Cappuccine church on the San Girolamo canal. La Maddalena sports an enigmatic, slightly sinister 'evil eye' motif on its circular Palladian façade, like some Masonic sign. San Marziale's bizarre high altar is a mad medley of jaundiced marble involving the world, the heavens and St Jerome.

Southeastern Cannaregio

The Strada Nova (New Street) is the main thoroughfare of this area, the broadest, straightest part of the route parallel to the Grand Canal between the railway station and the Rialto. Its creation in 1871 tore the stuffing out of the ancient labyrinthine alleys of Santa Fosca. Studded with old churches and the rear sides of waterfront palazzi, it still makes an interesting stroll. Look out for a wonderful antique chemist's shop at No. 2233, the Farmacia Santa Fosca, fitted with its original 17th-century dark-wood furnishings and majolica vases. Contrasting with the tawdry souvenirs of the Lista di Spagna further west, Strada Nova is an unpretentious shopping street selling the things Venetians habitually buy, from house wares to luscious cakes and stylish fashion. Wine bars, cafés and restaurants are plentiful. A dark side street leads to the **Ca' d'Oro**, one of the Grand Canal's most magnificent waterfront palaces.

Right: *Strada Nova, one of Venice's main shopping thoroughfares, was built during the Austrian occupation after knocking down many of the city's old houses.*

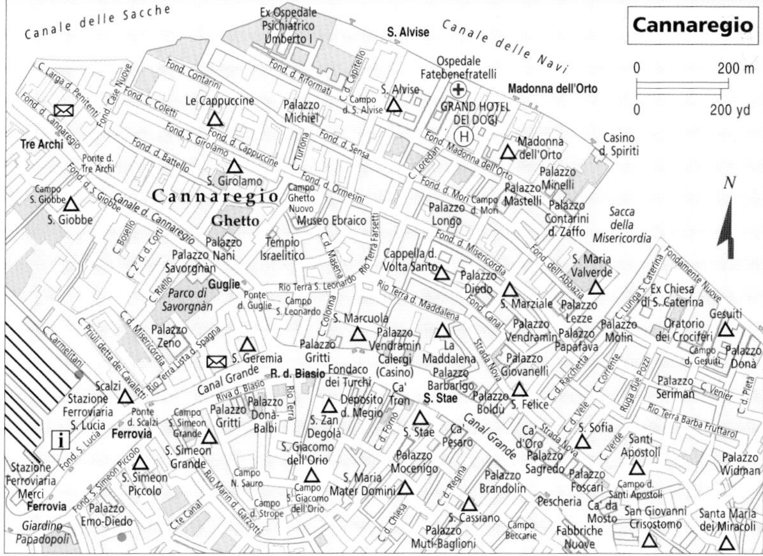

Ca' d'Oro ***

The lacy marble façade of this building overlooking the Grand Canal is one of the best examples of the Venetian Gothic style. Its name, 'House of Gold', refers to long-vanished gilding which must have made it a truly dazzling spectacle when it was first built in the early 15th century. It originally belonged to the Contarini family, a famous Venetian clan which produced no fewer than eight of the city's doges. After suffering dreadful indignities under later ownership, the palace was restored to something resembling its former glory in the early 20th century by the wealthy philanthropist and art collector Baron Giorgio Franchetti. He generously donated it to the state in 1915, along with its valuable contents of paintings, frescos, sculptures, ceramics and furniture.

The main prizes of the collection are Andrea Mantegna's *St Sebastian* (the artist's last work painted in 1506) and Tullio Lombardo's beautiful, broken-nosed *Double Portrait* sculpture. There are fine bronzes, important works by Carpaccio (*Annunciation* and *Death of the*

WHAT'S IN A NAME?

Two derivations of the name Cannaregio are widely circulated. A likely explanation is that it comes from the Canal Regio or Royal Canal (now called the Canale di Cannaregio), which was the main gateway to the city from the Italian mainland before the railway arrived. But some people claim it is based on the Italian word *canne*, meaning canes or reeds, which once grew in profusion on these marshy northern mud flats.

Virgin) and the Tuscan artist Luca Signorelli (*Flagellation*, ca. 1480), Venetian canal-scapes by Guardi, and a Titian *Venus*. The Flemish School is represented by Van Eyck and Memling, along with a priceless Dürer *Pietà*, and a charming 'Noah's Ark' tapestry. The intricately fretted loggias give excellent views over the Canal. A splendid carved wellhead by Bartolomeo Bon (one of Venice's best) can be seen in the paved courtyard. The palace is open daily, 08:15–14:00.

Aversion Therapy

Believe it or not, some people find Venice disappointing. This is how to have a bad time:

- Stay in a cheap hotel in Mestre or Marghera.
- Visit Venice on a tiring day trip, and cram too much in.
- Wear uncomfortable shoes.
- Try to see St Mark's at the same time as everyone else.
- Queue in hot sun or teeming rain to visit the Doge's Palace and the Accademia.
- Forget to check opening times before heading for a special museum or restaurant.
- Frequent tourist traps from San Marco to the Rialto.
- Have a *menu turistico* in an indifferent restaurant.
- Take a water-taxi or gondola without agreeing on a price.
- Join a trip to Murano's glass factories with a pushy tour guide wanting commission.
- Leave your bedroom windows open with the lights on during the mosquito season.

Santi Apostoli *

At a strategic junction of streets off the Strada Nova, this much-altered church makes more of a landmark than its architectural merits suggest. Inside, its most interesting feature is the 15th-century chapel to the right of the nave, which contains a Tiepolo (*The Communion of St Lucy*, 1748), and the dignified tomb of Marco Cornaro, possibly by Tullio Lombardo (1511). Cornaro's daughter Caterina briefly became Queen of Cyprus, and was buried here before being moved to the church of San Salvatore. Open Mon–Sat, 07:30–11:30 and 15:00–19:00.

San Giovanni Crisostomo *

One of the most atmospheric of Cannaregio's minor churches, this little terracotta-washed building is obviously a much-loved place of worship. Its Greek-cross interior feels cosy rather than gloomy – brightened with flowers and candles lit by parishioners who call in here on their way to work. Richly decorated inside, its most important work of art is a late painting by Giovanni Bellini (*St Jerome with Saints Christopher and Augustine*, 1513) on a side-altar to the right. The main altarpiece is by Sebastiano del Piombo (*St John Crysostom and Six Saints*, 1509–11). Open Mon–Sat 08:30–12:00 and 15:30–17:00; Sun 15:30–17:30.

Santa Maria dei Miracoli ***

A strong contender in the 'favourite Venetian church' list, this delightful early Renaissance building achieves almost universal acclaim, and makes a popular choice for Venetian weddings. Its creamy exterior, inset with gem-like roundels of coloured marble and exquisite architectural details, is often compared to a jewel box. It makes a cheering discovery, tucked away on a little island and mirrored by canals. Built in the 1480s by Pietro Lombardo, it houses a 'miraculous' *Madonna* painted by Nicolò di Pietro on its high altar. The interior is as sparkling as the outside, walls faced in polychrome panels and a barrel-vaulted ceiling studded with gilded portraits of saints and prophets. The galleried choir (which is used as a discreet entrance by nuns from the neighbouring convent) and balustrade beneath a starry apse are decorated with the delicate sculpture work for which the Lombardo family were renowned. The church is open Mon–Sat 09:00–17:00, Sun 13:00–17:00. Member of Chorus scheme (*see* page 20).

Chimneys

Cannaregio is a good place to see Venice's chimneypots, intended to reduce the risk of fire, a constant fear in this waterbound but built-up city. Designs varied from a sort of inverted flowerpot shape (to trap sparks) to capped cubes ringed by air holes.

Opposite: *The Ca' d'Oro makes a striking impact from the Grand Canal.*
Below: *The elaborate ceiling of Santa Maria dei Miracoli.*

Northern Cannaregio

North of Santa Maria dei Miracoli, a maze of narrow alleys trickles past workshops and artisan studios to the **Fondamente Nuove** (New Quays). No longer new (they date from the 1580s), these northern promenades lack the architectural distinction of the Riva degli Schiavoni or the Zattere, and can be windswept in winter. On the bustling quaysides, tides of passengers ebb and flow – visitors bound for the glassworks and lace shops of Murano and Burano, or Torcello's lovely churches. The terracotta walls of the cemetery island of San Michele are clearly visible across the water, a regular destination for Venetians in Grand Guignol

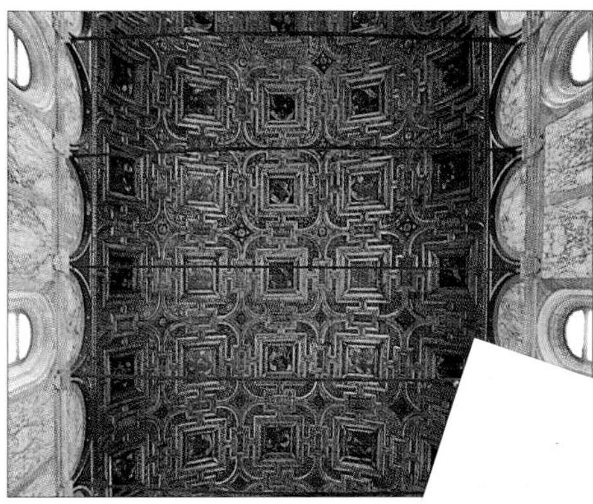

mourning garb, carrying flowers for departed loved ones. Local businesses adopt a pragmatic approach, specializing in marble-cutting and floristry for the undertaking trade. Lagoon views extend past San Michele's funereal cypresses to an alpine skyline. Not far behind the waterfront stands the imposing Jesuit temple of Santa Maria Assunta, better known as the **Gesuiti** church. A man-made basin called the Sacca della Misericordia takes a neat square bite out of northern Cannaregio, involving a trek inland if you are exploring on foot.

To the west of the Sacca della Misericordia, a poor but picturesque quarter surrounds the superb Gothic church of **Madonna dell'Orto**. Beyond lies the remote parish of **Sant'Alvise**, almost cut off by canals and frequently waterlogged. Peeling, shuttered houses decked with washing and topped with strangely shaped chimneys line these tranquil backwaters. Dotted amid humbler buildings, the battered façades of well-to-do mansions and neglected religious buildings stand, hoping for injections of conservation cash.

JESUIT KITSCH

The decorative effects of the Gesuiti church don't please everyone. 'In this dreary sanctuary is one of Titian's great paintings, *The Martyrdom of St Lawrence*, to which … you turn involuntarily, envious of the Saint toasting so comfortably on his gridiron amid all that frigidity … The workmanship is marvellously skilful, and the material costly, but it only gives the church the effect of being draped in damask linen … it is indescribably tableclothy …' (WD Howells, *Venetian Life*, 1866).

Gesuiti **

Venice's uneasy relationship with the Vatican made things difficult for the Jesuits during the 17th century, and it wasn't until 1714 that they finally obtained permission to build a church within the city. Its remote location is some indication of the suspicion with which this most Catholic of orders was still regarded. The Baroque building, gaunt and ponderous externally with great bronze doors and heavy Corinthian columns, is chiefly remarkable for its amazing interior, in which every surface seems to be smothered with green and white patterned fabric. These trompe l'œil effects are in fact achieved in solid inlaid marble, a virtuoso performance of decorative sculpture. The pulpit 'drapes' are

Below: *Flowers sold on Fondamente Nuove are destined for the cemetery of San Michele.*

especially breathtaking. Awesomely ugly barley-sugar pillars support a scaly dome over the high altar. Several important paintings in this church include Titian's *Martyrdom of St Lawrence* (1588, first altar on the left) a dramatic night scene showing the saint being barbecued with apparent equanimity. Open daily 10:00–12:00, 17:00–19:00.

Above: *Carved marble achieves astonishing fluidity in the Gesuiti church.*

Oratorio dei Crociferi *

Opposite the Gesuiti church, this building is the chapel of a hospice used by returning Crusaders during the 13th century, later an almshouse for the old and infirm. During the late 16th century the Oratory was decorated by Palma il Giovane with a series of paintings showing scenes from the history of its founders, the charitable order of the Crociferi (Bearers of the Cross). Following major flood damage in 1966, the building recently underwent extensive renovation funded by a number of conservation organizations. Open Thu–Sat 10:00–13:30.

Madonna dell'Orto ***

This lovely Gothic church dates from the 14th century. Its mellow red-brick façade is beautifully offset by pristine niched statuary and mini-spires of white stone. Set back on a broad square of herringbone paving, it makes a striking impact from the opposite side of the canal. The church was originally dedicated to St Christopher, patron of the ferrymen who carried passengers across the nearby lagoon. Later it was renamed Madonna of the Orchard (*orto*) after the miraculous appearance of a statue in a nearby garden. The church is particularly associated with Venetian painter Tintoretto, who lived a few yards away near the Campo dei Mori. His simple tomb lies in a chapel to the right of the altar. Several magnificent works by the artist surround the high altar, *The Last Judgement* (right), *The Sacrifice of the Golden Calf* (left) and *The Presentation of Mary at the Temple* (over the

Grappa

Near Asolo, the little town of Bassano del Grappa is famed for the fierce, clear spirit produced by distilling the skins and pips left after grapes have been pressed for wine. Grappa is a favourite after-dinner drink in the Veneto; shops sell many varieties beautifully packaged in glass flagons. One of the most famous producers is the old family firm of Nardini, based in Bassano del Grappa. Their small *bottega* near a covered timber bridge called the Ponte degli Alpini is a good place to try some before buying. The **Museo degli Alpini**, nearby, gives more information about grappa.

WELLS

Nearly every square in Venice contains a carved stone wellhead, now generally covered with a fixed iron lid. Reliable supplies of fresh water were essential before the days of piped water, and rules were stringent to prevent outbreaks of disease: 'beasts, unwashed pots and unclean hands' were forbidden. Wells were built above a clay-lined cistern filled with sand or gravel as a filter. Rain water was channelled into them from rooftop catchment areas. They were placed as high above the water table as possible to reduce salination in *acque alte* periods. Some of these wells are very beautiful. There are particularly fine ones in the courtyard of the Doge's Palace, and the Ca' d'Oro.

doorway on the right). A sad sign of modern times can be seen in the first chapel on the left. A faded photograph and empty frame are all that can be seen of Bellini's *Madonna and Child*, stolen in 1993. Open Mon–Sat 10:00–17:00, Sun 13:00–17:00. Member of Chorus scheme (*see* page 20).

Campo dei Mori **

This charming little square is named after the quaint stone carvings on its eastern side. These so-called 'Moors' (*Mori*) were alleged to represent the Mastelli brothers, silk merchants who settled in Venice from the Peloponnese (then known as Morea) during the early 12th century. Palazzo Mastelli, their canalside home, depicts a laden camel on its unusual façade. Just round the corner on the Rio della Sensa stands the modest house where Tintoretto spent the last two decades of his life with his daughter Marietta, also a talented artist.

Sant'Alvise *

Only determined sightseers track down this isolated church in the far north of the city. It has something of the air of a lumber-room, its contents stacked away from persistent rising damp. On the walls hangs a masterly collection of heartrending Tiepolos (*Road to Calvary; Flagellation; Crown of Thorns*), for once displayed at close quarters with enough light to see properly. The dizzying, riotously colourful trompe l'œil ceiling is a 17th-century double-act by Antonio Torri and Paolo Ricchi. The church is open Mon–Sat 10:00–17:00, Sun 15:00–17:00. Member of the Chorus scheme (*see* page 20).

Below: *A typical carved wellhead in Cannaregio.*

Central and Western Cannaregio

One of Cannaregio's most haunting neighbourhoods is the old Jewish quarter, the world's first **Ghetto**, where Shakespeare's Shylock would have been condemned to live, crammed with his co-religionists in tall, sunless terraces – the precursors of modern high-rises. In the far west of the area, around the eyecatching **Ponte dei Tre Archi**, on land reclaimed from reedy swamps, stand modern developments of imaginatively designed budget housing. The old slaughterhouse of Venice (Macello Pubblico) overlooking the lagoon is presently being used for university accommodation. To the south-west stands the city's huge railway station, Santa Lucia, expanded during the 1950s. Behind it stretches the 19th-century land-bridge called the **Ponte della Libertà**, skewering the floating city unromantically to the mainland. This somewhat humdrum road and rail link brings hordes of day-trippers to the city in July and August. A small tourist office within the station concourse caters for new arrivals.

The main route from the station to the city centre, the Lista di Spagna, is unenticingly packed with cheap hotels, mass-produced souvenirs and indifferent restaurants, but beyond the **Ponte delle Guglie** things improve with lively *bacari* (bars) and coffee shops. The Rio Terrà San Leonardo, a continuation of the main drag, was created by the Austrians during the 1870s by filling in an old canal. It links with the Strada Nova via the Maddalena district further to the east, through a series of atmospheric little squares dotted with churches. The only walkable stretch of Grand Canal lies immediately in front of the station, and the more attractive sections of Cannaregio's palatial waterfront can only be appreciated by boat. Prominent landmarks along these western reaches include the sallow-grey church of **San Geremia** (containing the relics of St Lucy), the blank pigeon ledges of **San Marcuola's** unfinished brick façade, and the Renaissance **Palazzo Vendramin Calergi**, where the composer Richard Wagner died in 1883. This building now houses the casino.

Above: *A quaint stone carving on Campo dei Mori.*

Il Milione

Marco Polo, born in Cannaregio around 1254, acquired his nickname *Il Milione* (Mr Million – referring to his supposed exaggerations) after the publication of his memoirs recounting nearly twenty years of fantastical adventures as a diplomat at the court of the Mongol emperor **Kublai Kahn**. Hardly anyone believed him, and he was begged to retract his wilder tales so that he could die in a state of grace. But Marco stuck to his guns, saying he had barely described half the wonders he had actually seen. The two little courtyards where his family lived are known as Corte Prima del Milion and Corte Seconda del Milion.

Above: *Quiet canalside buildings in Cannaregio.* **Opposite:** *These bronze reliefs by Arbit Blatas commemorate the 200 Venetian Jews deported during the Holocaust.*

The Ghetto ★★

The term which now denotes any confined ethnic community (especially Jewish ones) originated in Venice, and is a corruption of a Venetian-dialect word meaning foundry (*geto*), which occupied this part of Cannaregio in the 14th century. In 1516 the city authorities permitted large numbers of Jewish refugees from the Italian mainland to settle here, provided they confined themselves to a small island known as the Ghetto Nuovo. By day they were free to move anywhere, but they had to wear distinctive badges and clothing, and after the evening curfew the island was sealed off by guarded water gates. The marks left by the hinges of these massive barriers can still be seen in Sottoportego Ghetto Nuovo. As the population expanded, houses spread into the neighbouring Ghetto Vecchio, and additional storeys were built, turning these buildings into the tower blocks of their day. **Synagogues** (*scole*) for the various communities within the Ghetto were located on the top floors of the tenements. In 1797, Napoleon opened up the Ghetto, and today Venice's Jewish population of about 600 (about a tenth of what it was in the 17th century) is dispersed throughout the city. The last shameful chapter in the history of the Venetian Jews is recorded in seven **bronze plaques** commemorating 200 Holocaust victims.

The Ghetto's dilapidated, churchless streets and squares still hold strong cultural bonds for the Jewish community, and contain a traditional baker, bookshop, social centres and a kosher restaurant. The small **Museo Ebraico** outlines the history of the Jews in Venice, and displays Jewish ceremonial and sacred artefacts: ornate silver Torah covers, Hanukkah lamps and beautifully embroidered textiles. A solemn marriage contract

The White Lion

Near the Rialto on the Grand Canal is the **Ca' da Mosto**, birthplace of Alvise da Mosto, the explorer who discovered the Cape Verde Islands in the 15th century. For many years, the palace was occupied by a famous inn, the **Albergo del Leon Bianco**, known to Grand Tour visitors as The White Lion. In its heyday, while owned by Signor Petrillo, this was *the* place to stay in Venice: JMW Turner, Emperor Joseph II and the agronomist Arthur Young were all guests here. Since then the location has changed a couple of times, but Venice still has a Leon Bianco (*see* Where to Stay, page 117) occupying ancient premises next to the Ca' da Mosto.

(*ketubah*) makes touching reading, the bridegroom promising all his worldly goods 'even including the cloak off my back...'. Open Sun–Fri, Jun–Sept 10:00–19:00, Oct–May 10:00–16:30. Guided tours of the five synagogues (otherwise inaccessible) can be arranged on an inclusive ticket.

San Giobbe *

Visitors familiar with Tuscany may recognize the distinctive glazed terracotta work of the Della Robbia family decorating a chapel in the left-hand aisle – Venice's sole example. This little-known parish church tucked away in the far west of Cannaregio also contains an altar dedicated to the city's boatmen (Christ walks on the waters, using his Cross much like a gondolier's oar). Disgruntled, comical-looking lions support the tomb of Renato de Voyer, a former French ambassador who died in Venice in 1651. Hidden in the sacristy is one of Vivarini's lustrous triptychs. Notice the fine sculptured saints over the main doorway, by Pietro Lombardo. Open Mon–Sat, 10:00–12:00 and 15:00–18:00.

Terrazo alla Veneziana

Venice's unstable, waterlogged terrain creates an insurance company's nightmare scenario of heave and subsidence. One way of dealing with floors that ripple and lift like the waves of the lagoon is to lay down an aggregate mixture of crushed marble chips and plaster, which is both more elastic and more easily repaired than solid blocks of stone or marble. These mottled floor-coverings can be seen in many buildings in Venice. They are treated annually with linseed oil to keep them bright and supple.

Scalzi *

On the waterfront beside the railway station is the church of Santa Maria di Nazareth, better known as the Scalzi after the barefoot Carmelite friars who commissioned it during the 1670s. The clumsy-looking Baroque interior was designed by Baldassare Longhena, with gloomy salami-coloured walls and lumpish spiral altar columns. An Austrian bomb destroyed its Tiepolo ceiling frescos in 1915 (possibly its best feature), since replaced by a modern work by Ettore Tito (*The Council of Ephesus*). Open Mon–Sat, 09:30–12:00 and 15:30–18:00; Sun 15:30–17:30.

5
Santa Croce and San Polo

Together, these small *sestieri* form a compact fan shape, tucked into the goose-necked northern bend of the Grand Canal. Santa Croce is the only Venetian district accessible by road. The bus station makes an unlovely if necessary intrusion opposite the railway station in **Piazzale Roma**. Expensive parking space is provided in a multi-storey shed at the end of the Ponte della Libertà (the road link to Mestre). Don't despair if this is your first landfall in central Venice. A short walk through gardens and over narrow bridges soon leads to much more enticing areas. Several of Santa Croce's grander buildings contain museums. Its tiny maze-like back-streets are quieter than many of Venice's beaten tracks – ideal for an unscheduled wander, getting pleasantly lost and soaking up atmosphere. It is also a good area to look for a decent pizza – not easily found elsewhere in Venice.

For a more focused approach to sightseeing, try picking a route past some of its minor churches. There are too many to describe individually, but most deserve a glance. The demolished church which gave the *sestiere* its name once stood on the site occupied by the Giardini Papadopoli. From here, thread past the stern neo-Classical church of San Nicolò da Tolentino to San Simeon Piccolo and San Simeon Grande near the Grand Canal, finishing at Santa Maria Mater Domini's pretty square. Further afield, the boundary between Santa Croce and San Polo isn't obvious, but if you spot the **Rialto Bridge** or the huge church of the **Frari**, you'll know you've reached the lively *sestiere* of San Polo, the trading centre of ancient mercantile Venice.

Don't Miss

*** **Ponte di Rialto:** this is the Grand Canal's most famous bridge, a thoroughfare of jewellers' shops and amazing views.
*** **Frari church:** after the Basilica di San Marco, the Frari is Venice's largest and most impressive church.
*** **Scuola Grande di San Rocco:** a dazzling showcase of Tintoretto's works.
** **Rialto markets:** the Pescheria (fish market) and the Erberia (produce market) are always a lively sight on weekday mornings.

Opposite: *Ponte di Rialto is a scene of constant activity on and above the water line.*

Bridges

Piazzale Roma is surrounded by an extraordinary number of bridges. From the Tre Ponti on its southeastern corner (where there are actually five interlocking bridges, not three), you can see a dozen other bridges simultaneously – more than anywhere else in Venice. Yet another bridge is on the drawing board to cross the Grand Canal diagonally from Piazzale Roma to Santa Lucia station, though on grounds of cost and environmental impact it hasn't yet been given the go-ahead.

The Grand Canal

Santa Croce and San Polo enjoy a longer combined stretch of **Grand Canal** frontage than any other single Venetian district. Only certain sections near the bridges can be seen on foot, so a boat trip is a must at some stage. *Vaporetto* No. 1 (the *Accelerato*), or a more leisurely but expensive gondola ride, gives you the opportunity to spot the monuments between Piazzale Roma and San Tomà. This includes not just Santa Croce and San Polo, but the whole of Cannaregio's Grand Canal waterfront, and half of San Marco's too. Boats pass beneath two of the Canal's three bridges, the **Scalzi** and the **Rialto**. Among the stately palazzi displaying variations on Veneto-Byzantine, Gothic, Renaissance and Baroque themes, the pinnacled Palazzo Belloni Battagia or the crimson doll's house once known as the Casa Favretto (now the Hotel San Cassiano) may catch your eye. The diorama rolls on past churches, warehouses, markets and quaysides. Take the camera, choose an outer seat on the prow, and get snapping.

Fondaco dei Turchi *

The 'Turks' Warehouse' makes a striking statement just opposite the *vaporetto* station of San Marcuola. This imposing Veneto-Byzantine building was built in 1250 as a private dwelling. From 1621 to 1838 it functioned as the headquarters of the Ottoman trade delegation, bringing a whiff of eastern promise to the wharves of the Grand Canal with its exotic cargoes of rice, silks and spices. In addition, the building also provided the Muslim community with a mosque, bathhouse and bazaar. Later abandoned when Oriental trade declined, it fell into ruin and was heavily and unsympathetically restored by the Austrians in the 19th century. Today it houses Venice's

Below: *The multiple horseshoe arches of the Fondaco dei Turchi make it one of the Grand Canal's most easily spotted façades.*

natural history museum (**Museo di Storia Naturale**), currently closed for yet more long-term restoration. The crenellated brick building next to it is the **Deposito del Megio**, a storehouse that was once kept stocked with an emergency supply of grain for the city.

San Stae *

The graceful façade of this Baroque church set slightly back from the waterfront on a paved terrace marks a pleasing change of gear from the style of the palaces all around it. It dates from 1709, funded by a doge's legacy, and its name is a typically Venetian distortion of Sant'Eustachio. Its bright, streamlined interior makes a good foil for occasional exhibitions and concerts, but its walls hold some noteworthy permanent works by Tiepolo, Ricci and Piazzetta. Look out for the grisly *memento mori* in the central marble floor panel. Open Mon–Sat 10:00–17:00; Sun 13:00–17:00. A member of the Chorus scheme (*see* page 20).

Ca' Pesaro *

One of the Grand Canal's more startling façades belongs to this majestic Baroque palace of white marble designed by Baldassare Longhena. It was completed in 1710, and features a curved array of grotesque masks leering amid seemly Classical columns, balustrades and arches, its ground floor ribbed with spiky chevron

Biasio the Butcher

The stretch of waterfront and *vaporetto* station known as the Riva di Biasio near San Simeon Grande is associated with a grisly tale. A local butcher named Biasio was sentenced to death after it was discovered that some of the meat he was selling in his shop was human flesh. He was publicly beheaded between the columns of the Piazzetta San Marco. Posthumous urban myth turned him into the Sweeney Todd of Venice; it is said he made children into sausages.

Above: *Boats glide past the palaces of the Grand Canal.*

Palazzo Mocenigo

A couple of blocks behind the waterfront from San Stae is the battered 17th-century Palazzo Mocenigo, bearing the name of an august Venetian family. Seven doges were Mocenigos (some are buried in the church of Santi Giovanni e Paolo). Furnished in authentic 18th-century style, the palazzo houses a small collection of antique fabrics and costumes. The interior offers a glimpse of Venetian high-life, surrounded by portraits of the great and famous, Murano chandeliers and frescoed ceilings. Open Tue–Sat 10:00–17:00.

patterns. It took over 50 years to build, and seems to be taking just as long to renovate, but is destined, eventually, to hold two museums. Determined visitors can tiptoe through a dusty building site and up long flights of steps to visit the **Museo d'Arte Orientale**, a collection of curios assembled by the Conti di Bardi on his extensive travels in the Far East. The quality of this horde of samurai armour, porcelain, netsuke, batik and painted screens is indisputable, but as yet it is disappointingly displayed in ill-lit and poorly labelled surroundings. Open Tue–Sun 09:00–14:00. The **Galleria d'Arte Moderna** (modern art museum) contains 19th- and 20th-century works (still closed for restoration). At least the canal views from the top floors of this fine palace are worth the climb.

Around the Rialto

Very few landmarks are as instantly recognizable as the crook-backed **Ponte di Rialto**, spanning the Grand Canal at one of its tightest turns. The present bridge dates only from the 16th century, but a crossing point has existed here ever since Venice's earliest days. Legend has it that the city's first inhabitants took refuge on the small islands known as the Rivus Altus ('high bank') or Rialto, safely above the fluctuating water line of the lagoon. By the Middle Ages, this area had become the nerve centre of a rapidly developing maritime trading empire. A number of wharves and warehouses sprang up all along its banks to accommodate a bewildering range of cargoes that came in from far and wide: jewels and precious metals, textiles and spices, dyes and perfumes. Wine-casks were unloaded along the **Riva del Vin**, which is today a broad esplanade of pavement restaurants and gondola stands. Shops, taverns and inns spilled into the narrow alleys behind the waterfront, and **markets** selling anything and everything stretched along the busy quaysides. For centuries, this was the best place to find out how the world turned: 'What news on the Rialto?' (*The Merchant of Venice*).

Recognizing a business opportunity when they saw one, the city's canny financiers set up Europe's first state bank here, which soon took on the role of an international Bourse, controlling currency exchanges throughout the trading world between the 12th and the 16th centuries. The chancy wheels of commerce were oiled by wealthy Jewish money-lenders and entrepreneurial merchant-venturers – the Shylocks and Antonios of Renaissance Venice. At the other end of the social spectrum, mountebanks, charlatans and astonishing numbers of prostitutes plied their trade in this crowded cosmopolitan quarter. Today, the quays, shops and markets of the Rialto are as lively and colourful as ever, a jostling interface of native Venetians and foreign visitors exchanging greetings, goods and gossip throughout the day.

Traghetti

'Bring them, I pray thee,
with imagined speed
Unto the traject, to the
common ferry
Which trades to Venice ...'
(Portia, *The Merchant of Venice*)

San Polo and Santa Croce are starting points for five of the Grand Canal's seven ferry gondola routes, or *traghetti*, which ply the canal from special piers. With set fares costing under L1000, this is by far the cheapest way to experience a gondola ride. It is customary to stand during the crossing, so make sure you are carefully balanced, with a firm grip on your possessions, especially when embarking and disembarking.

Below: Traghetti *(ferry gondolas) hop back and forth across the canal.*

Street Traders

Some of the quaint old streets near the Rialto retain the names of the trades once associated with them. Calle Casaria belonged to the cheesemongers, Saoneri to the soap-makers, Speziali to the spice-sellers, Cordaria to the rope-makers, Orefici to the goldsmiths, Cappeller to the milliners and Botteri to the coopers or barrel-makers. The Ponte delle Tette gained its raunchily guessable name from the topless prostitutes who displayed their wares near this red-light bridge in the 14th century.

Ponte di Rialto ***

The present stone structure replaced a series of earlier wooden bridges which either collapsed or were washed away. It was built over a three-year period between 1588 and 1591, and its ambitious single span of white marble required stabilizing with an enormous number of foundation piles driven into the marshy ground. The architect who won the competitive tender for this very prestigious commission beat the heavyweights of his day like Michelangelo, Palladio and Sansovino – perhaps because of his fortuitous name, Antonio da Ponte. Whatever the reason, his unusual design, high enough at its midpoint to enable galley masts to pass through, has stood the test of time. A double row of shops surmounts it (these are mostly jewellers and goldsmiths), and its balustraded walkways offer breathtaking vistas of the Grand Canal. Until 1854, when the Accademia bridge was completed, this was the only point at which the Canal could be crossed on foot. It is still by far the most well-used bridge in Venice, constantly thronged with tourists. Souvenir sellers ambush passers-by on the San Polo side of the bridge.

Below: *Gondolas compete for space with many other watercraft on the canal near the Rialto Bridge.*

Rialto Markets **

Seen from the waters of the Grand Canal, the pink-and-white Gothic porticoes of the market hall cut a dash on the broad quays of the **Pescheria**, where seafood arrives by barge before dawn (Tue–Sat). Crates of gleaming squid and countless other fishy species take their last gasp on fern-lined counters; hapless crustaceans feebly waving pincers and antennae. Nearby are the colourful fruit and vegetable stalls of the **Erberia**, a cornucopia of produce from all over the Veneto (Mon–Sat). This photogenic scene is at its best in the early morning; by midday, the traders start to go home. Close to the Rialto Bridge stands a large complex of arcaded buildings called the **Fabbriche Nuove** and **Fabbriche Vecchie**, formerly used as administrative offices for the market. They date from 1514, when a disastrous fire destroyed virtually everything in the area (the canals were frozen in this exceptionally icy winter, so couldn't be used to extinguish the flames).

San Giacomo di Rialto *

Claimed to be one of the oldest churches in Venice, San Giacometto, as it is affectionately known by the local people, has been a great spiritual focus for the Rialto community ever since Medieval times. A variety of mercantile guilds, such as the goldsmiths and the cheese-sellers, donated funds for the upkeep of the church, and commissioned the altars inside. The present building is believed to date from the 12th century. Its most distinctive feature is undoubtedly its enormous, eccentric-looking 24-hour clock-face, with just a single golden hand which, since its installation, has hardly ever shown the correct time. The Gothic exterior portico is another unusual aspect of the church. The interior shows Byzantine influences, with the Greek-cross plan of many early Venetian churches. An apt inscription is carved round the exterior of the apse: 'Around this temple, let the merchant's law be just, his weights true, and his promises faithful'. This church is open daily 10:30–12:00; Mon–Sat 16:00–17:30.

Picnic Food

The Rialto markets are an excellent place to collect picnic supplies, perfect for a lagoon outing, or to enjoy in public squares and gardens. Use steps or wellheads as tables and chairs if there are no benches. Salads and fruit can be found in the Erberia, while Ruga Rialto's appetizing food shops sell a terrific range of regional cheeses, cold meats, bread and mouth-watering cakes. Try the baker called **Mauro** at No. 603, the delicatessen called **Aliani** at 654, and the cheese shop **Latteria Ronchi Francesco** at 1053a. Alternatively, head for one of the snack bars near Piazzale Roma for ready-made *panini* or *tramezzini*, or buy a take-away pizza or *calzone* from **Pizzeria d'Asporto**, at Salizzado San Rocco 3034 (just behind the Frari).

Above: *The candlelit interior of Santa Maria Gloriosa dei Frari.*

The Frari District

Away from the Grand Canal, there is a lot to see. The main highlights are the wonderful church of **Santa Maria Gloriosa dei Frari**, and the spectacular **Scuola Grande di San Rocco**, respectively the city's greatest church (after San Marco) and its greatest *scuola*. Other delights include the Campo San Polo, one of the city's largest squares, and a clutch of fascinating churches. Most rewarding of these is perhaps **San Giacomo dell'Orio**, a focal point in Santa Croce. Many visitors, however, find this district just as enticing for its shops and restaurants as for its sights. Wonderful boutiques, less pricy and commercialized than those near San Marco or the Rialto, line the streets near the Frari. This is a good place to look for presents, with a variety of stationery, scarves, bags, toys, textiles and carnival costumes on sale.

Scuole

A Venetian *scuola* (from *schola*, a guild or corporation) was a charitable association or club set up under the aegis of a patron saint to undertake philanthropic duties like health care or looking after families who fell on hard times. These lay confraternities, together with the local church, formed the social and religious framework of the community. The Big Six were known as the Scuole Grandi, but there were once literally hundreds in the city, many run by workers' guilds. Bequests and donations made some of them hugely rich, able to acquire magnificent buildings and priceless artworks at the expense of their intended beneficiaries. They were eventually suppressed under Napoleonic rule.

Santa Maria Gloriosa dei Frari ***

The contents of this huge Gothic church make it one of Venice's most impressive sacred places. A Franciscan building (*frari* means friars), it was founded in about 1250, about the same time as Santi Giovanni e Paolo (San Zanipolo, *see* page 49), with which it is often compared. Though a shade smaller than its Dominican rival in Castello, the Frari is perhaps more satisfying inside. The present structure was begun in the 14th century (a lengthy project which took over a century – the tall campanile was completed in 1396). The red-brick exterior is gaunt and rather uninspiring; it is the inside that impresses, the colossal shell illumined by jewel-like windows, glorious works of art, startling monuments, and also a splendidly carved Monk's Choir in three tiers, showing bas-reliefs of saints and city scenes.

Pride of place is taken by Titian's *Assumption of the Virgin* (1518) over the high altar, a vivid example of his dramatic use of light and colour (red!). A second Titian masterpiece, *Madonna di Ca' Pesaro* (1526), hangs to the left of the main door. Equally impressive, but a world away in style, are Bellini's contemplative *Madonna and Child with Saints* (1488) and Vivarini's altarpiece in the Bernardo Chapel. Elsewhere you can spot Donatello's wooden sculpture of *John the Baptist* (ca. 1450), the rood screen by Pietro Lombardo and Bartolomeo Bon (1475), and the Corner Chapel. Important tombs commemorate several Venetian doges and the composer Monteverdi, but the most memorable monuments are an extraordinary pyramidal one for Canova (containing the sculptor's heart) and a grandiose neo-Classical horror for Titian, designed by some of his pupils. Titian died of the plague in 1576, and was the only victim in Venice to be allowed a church burial during this frightful epidemic. Open Mon–Sat 09:00–18:00; Sun 13:00–18:00. Member of Chorus scheme (*see* page 20).

THE RIALTO HUNCHBACK

At the back of the square on which the church of San Giacomo di Rialto stands is a small 16th-century statue of a man bent double under his burdens, called the **Gobbo** (hunchback) **di Rialto**. From the flight of steps he carries on his back, various Venetian decrees were promulgated and public announcements made. As a punishment, convicted petty criminals were forced to run naked from Piazza San Marco to this statue through a hail of blows and insults from onlookers.

Scuola Grande di San Rocco ***

A few paces from the Frari's apse is San Polo's second highlight, greatest of the Venetian *scuole* and an absolute must for any art-lover. You will find a great number of fine works by Tintoretto scattered throughout the churches of the city, but this is without question the best collection of the artist's work under one roof. This *scuola* was founded in 1478 as a hospice for the sick after an outbreak of the plague. St Roch (San Rocco) of

Below: *The Scuola Grande di San Rocco, a treasure-house of Tintoretto's work.*

Carlo Goldoni

Venice's best-known playwright began his career as a lawyer, but wrote part-time for the Commedia dell'Arte, a popular dramatic form of the day, featuring the masked characters Harlequin and Columbine. Later in life he began writing sharper social and political satires. He moved to Paris in 1762, and taught Italian at the court of Louis XVI, but became caught up in the events of the French Revolution and lost his royal pension. His output was prolific; he once won a bet that he could produce a play a week for an entire year.

Montpellier was chosen as its patron because he had worked among plague victims, and had himself apparently been cured of this dread disease by a dog which licked his sores.

The building has two floors, the lower reception hall splendid enough, but just an appetizer for the amazing upper floor, once used for confraternity meetings. The walls and ceilings glow with 54 of Tintoretto's masterly works. The Great Hall upstairs contains Old and New Testament scenes, many devoted to the healing miracles of Christ. Beneath the paintings are a series of allegorical carvings by the sculptor Francesco Pianta, including a caricature of Tintoretto. A side room on the upper floor houses what many consider Tintoretto's greatest (certainly it is his largest) painting, *The Crucifixion*. The small oval ceiling painting in this room is believed to be the one which won Tintoretto his commission (*see* panel, page 77). The lower hall is decorated with later canvasses which focus on scenes from the life of the Virgin. The rooms are rather dark, but hand-held mirrors are provided to help visitors avoid too much of a crick in the neck. Open daily 09:00–17:30.

The church of **San Rocco**, located on the same square, is a mainly 18th-century building containing more of Tintoretto's works depicting scenes from the life of St Roch, predictably curing plague victims. Open Mon–Sat 07:30–12:30 and 15:00–17:00; Sun 08:00–12:30.

Below: *Giovanni Bellini's altarpiece in the Frari church depicts the Virgin and Child flanked by saints.*

Campo San Polo **

This large open space has witnessed many spectacles, from bullfights and masked balls to a notorious assassination. In 1548 Lorenzo de Medici took refuge in Venice after killing his cousin, the Duke of Florence. Revenge followed, and Lorenzo was stilettoed by hired killers. Today Campo San Polo seems

Left: *Handcarts are sometimes the only practical way to move heavy baggage around many Venetian streets.*

a more peaceful place fringed by pavement cafés, a haunt of skate-boarding or ball-playing children most evenings, and sometimes a venue for concerts, carnivals or open-air film shows. Its fountain (Venice has very few of these) makes an interesting focal point. Several Gothic palaces flank the square, notably Palazzo Soranzo and Palazzo Corner Mocenigo. The ancient church of San Polo at its southwestern corner has a striking Gothic portal of coloured marble. It contains works by Veronese and Palma il Giovane, a fine cycle of Tiepolo Stations of the Cross, and also a *Last Supper* by Tintoretto. The two lions at the base of its bell tower hold a serpent and a human head (symbolizing that of the decapitated Doge Falier) between their paws. Open Mon–Sat 10:00–17–00; Sun 13:00–17:00. Member of Chorus scheme (*see* page 20).

San Giacomo dell'Orio **

Back in Santa Croce again, this ornate early church is full of charm and interest. Features survive from various eras: the campanile, Greek cross plan and Byzantine capitals (notice the *verde antico* of green marble) date from the 13th century, while the magnificent ship's-keel ceiling, Gothic nave columns and rounded apses are from later periods. Notice the fine old font and pulpit, and the wooden sculpture of the Virgin waving (left of the main altar). Ceiling paintings by Veronese in the sacristy, and a late Lotto altarpiece *Madonna and Four Saints* are among its art treasures. Open Mon–Sat 10:00–17:00; Sun 13:00–17:00. Member of Chorus scheme (*see* page 20).

Tintoretto's Trick

When the Scuola Grande di San Rocco was completed, the best artists of the day were invited to enter a competition to decide who would win the prestigious commission of an inaugural picture. Instead of submitting a sketch plan as requested, Tintoretto bribed an accomplice to fix a finished painting in the spot where it was destined to hang – concealed by a curtain. When his turn came to show a sketch, he pulled a rope to unveil the completed canvas. Jaws dropped all round, and of course, Tintoretto won the prize, much to the resentment of his fellow artists. For the next 25 years, commissions rolled in, and this project became his first priority.

6
Dorsoduro

This southerly *sestiere* frames the Grand Canal's final meander through Venice, piercing the San Marco basin in a sharpened hook at one of the city's most striking landmarks, the church of **Santa Maria della Salute**. Dorsoduro is many people's favourite part of Venice. One of the earliest settlement points, the name means 'hard spine', referring to the solid clay subsoil of its once separate islands, which lay well above the lagoon and provided firmer foundations for building than the rest of Venice. Full of historic interest, quiet and picturesque in parts, Venice's 'Left Bank' is also very lively and slightly bohemian, the site of three major art galleries and a raffish café scene. Wealthy expatriates, including American copper heiress Peggy Guggenheim, chose to settle in its favoured eastern sectors, taking advantage of idyllic waterfront views. The Anglican church of St George was established to cater for its Protestant community.

Other parts of Dorsoduro, at least in former days, were very poor. The parish of San Nicolò dei Mendicoli and the Malcanton district were closely associated with beggars and footpads, and had a higher crime rate than the rest of the city. Relics of the Industrial Revolution (cotton-mills, storehouses and gas tanks) still dramatize the skyline of Dorsoduro's westerly working-class neighbourhoods. Today, a programme of urban renewal involving public works and new housing schemes has revitalized these once rather run-down city fringes, where tourists scarcely ventured, into flourishing dockland and university zones.

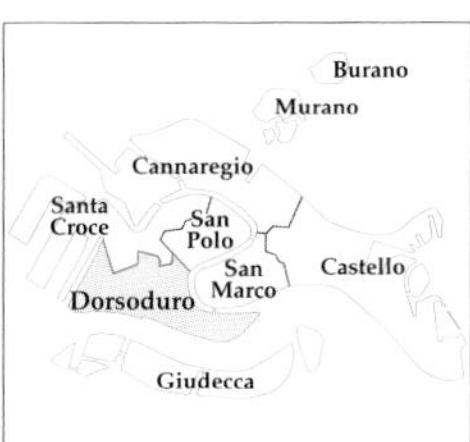

Don't Miss

***** Galleria dell'Accademia:** Venice's foremost art gallery, a distillation of over six centuries of Venetian painting.
***** Collezione Guggenheim:** thought-provoking contemporary art, stylishly displayed in a delightful garden setting.
***** Santa Maria della Salute:** Baroque splendour at entrance to the Grand Canal.
**** San Nicolò dei Mendicoli:** a charming minor church, magnificently restored.
**** Campo Santa Margherita:** lively square, full of cafés and market stalls.

Opposite: *Santa Maria della Salute at the southerly end of the Grand Canal.*

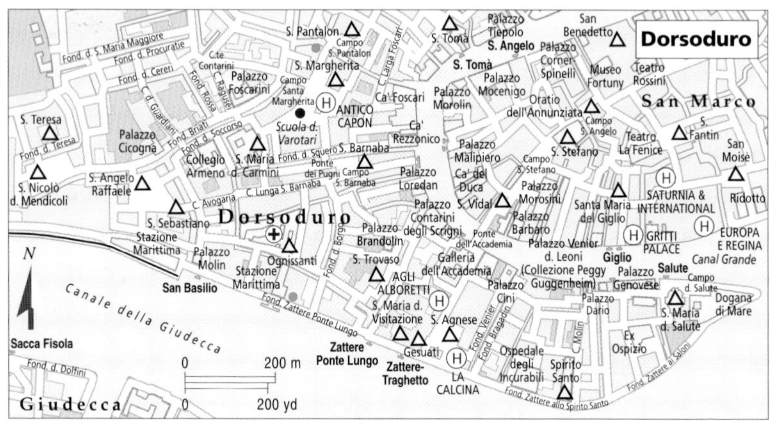

Cruise liners and cargo vessels berth at the commercial port. Most visitors to Dorsoduro approach the area from the direction of San Marco via the **Ponte dell'Accademia**, an old wooden bridge which was originally built as a temporary measure in the 19th century, and which has somehow never been replaced. Located immediately beyond the Ponte dell'Accademia is the area's premier tourist attraction, the **Galleria dell'Accademia**.

> **DON'T LOOK NOW**
>
> Visitors catching sight of the remote church of San Nicolò dei Mendicoli may experience a *frisson* of unease if they have ever seen Nick Roeg's film *Don't Look Now*, based on an eerie tale by Daphne du Maurier. This little building, and the once run-down neighbourhood surrounding it, provided atmospheric location shots for this 1970s movie. San Nicolò's 12th-century bell tower was the scene of the film's spine-chilling climax, which rivals the famous shower scene in Hitchcock's *Psycho* as a memorably horrifying moment in cinematic history.

A Venetian Art Trail

Within ten minutes' walk of the Ponte dell'Accademia lie three of the city's best art collections. Take note of the opening times: the galleries have different closing days. Waterfront views are archetypal around the bridge, a popular vantage point for artists and photographers. The main street linking the three galleries is amply stocked with *trattorie* and stylish little boutiques selling high-quality versions of the crafts for which Venice is famous, such as elaborate stationery and hand-blocked textiles.

Galleria dell'Accademia ★★★

Essential viewing for any understanding of Venetian painting, this gallery was established by Napoleon in 1807 (Venice has some reason at least to thank the Little Emperor). The core of the collection consists of the contents of the Accademia di Belle Arti, an 18th-century institution founded by the artist Piazzetta. It was much expanded by additional works from churches and monasteries Napoleon had suppressed. One such deconsecrated convent was La Carita, which now houses the Accademia.

The contents range from the Byzantine and Gothic periods through the High Renaissance to Baroque and 18th-century works. All the great Venetians are represented in this collection, from Carpaccio and Bellini, through Giorgione and Veronese to Tintoretto, Titian and Tiepolo. The riches now on show represent only a tiny fraction of the wealth of art that Venice once possessed, most of which has been stolen or sold off through the centuries.

A tour through the 24 rooms in numerical order takes you in a roughly chronological loop from the earliest Venetian painters through the Renaissance to landscapes and genre paintings of the 18th century, then back to the Renaissance again for two great fresco cycles in the final rooms. These ambitious ceremonial paintings end the visit on a high note. Temporary special exhibitions may disrupt the locations of certain paintings, and attract larger crowds than usual. In high summer, arrive early or time your visit around lunchtime, when the queues shorten.

Room 1 is the gilded chapterhouse of La Carita's former *scuola*, with two glowing stylized portrayals of *The Coronation of the Virgin*. One is by an early master of the Venetian School, Paolo Veneziano, still showing Byzantine influences; the other is a Gothic work by Michele Giambono. By the time this second work was completed (1448) the Renaissance was in full swing, and Venice was experiencing an artistic flowering similar to that of Florence, Siena and Rome. Foremost among the artists of this period were Andrea

Distressed Gentlefolk

During the 18th century, dozens of *declassé* aristocrats who had fallen on hard times swarmed into the cheap lodgings around San Barnaba and became known as the Barnabotti. Too proud to earn a living by trade, they supported themselves by selling their votes to the Maggior Consiglio, or subsisted on meagre state pensions. But no matter how poor they were, they always dressed in silk, an obligation of their social status.

Below: *Lace in many different forms was once an important Venetian export commodity.*

Mantegna and the Bellini family; some fine examples of their work are on display in Rooms 2–5. Giovanni Bellini's *Madonna and Child Enthroned* and *Pietà* are especially beautiful. Cima da Conegliano, Carpaccio and the Vivarini brothers are also represented in these first five rooms. Two artists who chose non-religious subjects are given high-profile wall space further on. Giorgione's enigmatic *Tempest* (ca. 1507) and his *Portrait of an Old Woman* stand next to each other in a separate enclave; Lorenzo Lotto's *Gentleman in his Study* (ca. 1525) is a haunting example of Renaissance psychological portraiture (notice the lizard on his desk).

The High Renaissance rolls on with big hitters like Paolo Veronese, whose vast canvas called *A Feast in the House of Levi* (1573) aroused the attention of the Inquisition. Its subject matter (dwarfs, drunkards, dogs, and above all Germans, tainting the scene with scandalous whiffs of Lutheranism) was considered too profane for its original title (*The Last Supper*). Veronese cheerfully agreed to change the name, and all was well. Venice's greatest painters dominate the next few rooms. Tintoretto is represented by several paintings on the theme of St Mark which helped to establish his reputation: *St Mark Freeing a Slave* (1548), *The Stealing of St Mark's Body*. Titian's late *Pietà* (1576) is one of the most striking works in this central section, but his *pièce de résistance* in the Accademia is the *Presentation of the Virgin* (1538) displayed in the gallery's final room, the Sala dell'Albergo.

Later sections wind down gently through lesser Baroque works, followed by calm landscapes and scenes of Venice by Guardi. There are even a couple of Canalettos (whose paintings of the Grand Canal are oddly

Wild Abandon

The Palazzo Venier dei Leoni seems to have inspired excess throughout its history. The original Venier owners kept a pet lion chained in the garden during the 18th century, and the Marchesa Casati held outrageously decadent parties here in the early 20th century, spraying the gardens with lilac paint and installing naked 'slaves', wildcats, apes and Afghan hounds to liven up the proceedings. Some of the goings-on in Peggy's day also raised eyebrows. She was apparently in the habit of unscrewing the *Angel of the City*'s most prominent feature and presenting it to nonplussed male guests.

rare in Venice). Tiepolo is the major Venetian artist of the 18th century, represented here by the fragments rescued from the Scalzi church after it was hit by a bomb in 1915.

Interest ratchets up several gears for a final crescendo in Rooms 20 and 21 with the astonishing cycle of paintings called *The Miracles of the True Cross*, commissioned for the Scuola di San Giovanni Evangelista, and executed by Vittorio Carpaccio and Gentile Bellini. In the next room, another series of related paintings by Carpaccio, recounting *Scenes from the Legend of St Ursula* (ca. 1490). These very vivid tableaux contain masses of architectural detail and costumes revealing life in 15th-century Venice. One (*The Healing of the Madman*, 1496) shows the old Rialto Bridge which collapsed in 1524 – notice the flared chimneypots designed to reduce the risk of fire. Open Mon 09:00–14:00, Tue–Sun 08:15–19:15 (hours vary seasonally; guided tours in English Wed and Thu 10:00, 11:00, 12:00). A combined ticket is available including Ca' d'Oro and the Oriental Museum.

Opposite: *This* bocca di leone *denunciation box on the Zattere was once used for citizens' complaints.* **Below:** *Marino Marini's striking modern sculpture arrests attention at the Guggenheim Collection.*

Palazzo Cini **

A private collection is housed in the Palazzo Cini, just a couple of blocks east along the waterfront from the Accademia. It was assembled by the art-lover Count Vittorio Cini (1884–1977) as a memorial to his son who was killed in a plane crash. Fine artefacts on display include silver, ivories, porcelain and furniture, but the main interest is a valuable horde of Tuscan and Ferrarese paintings by early Renaissance masters such as Piero della Francesca, Botticelli, Filippo Lippi and Piero di Cosimo. Opening hours may be erratic, depending on temporary exhibitions. Open Tue–Sun, summer only, 10:00–13:00 and 14:00–18:00.

Palazzo Dario

There's no mistaking this delightful 15th-century palace from the Grand Canal. Its arched Renaissance façade of 'clockface' coloured marbles topped with torch-like chimneys is a dazzler. It backs on to the tiny, tree-lined square of Campiello Barbaro, near the Guggenheim Collection. Despite its cheering appearance, this pretty building has an unhappy history. Ill luck seems to have dogged its inhabitants in the shape of suicide, murder and financial ruin. Latest in this tragic catalogue was prominent Italian industrialist Raul Gardini, who shot himself in 1985.

Collezione Peggy Guggenheim ***

In a completely different key from the Accademia, but every bit as enjoyable, the Peggy Guggenheim Collection of contemporary art is one of the most visited museums in Venice. A large part of its attraction rests in its setting in the off-beat Palazzo Venier dei Leoni, presiding over an enviable expanse of Grand Canal waterfront. This building consists of just the ground floor of a gleaming white 18th-century palazzo – the rest was never completed. Its surreal architecture and flamboyant history no doubt appealed to the American heiress Peggy Guggenheim (1898–1979), who purchased the palace in 1949 and lived here until her death 30 years later. A great patron of avant-garde art, she embarked on an ambitious programme of collecting from the 1930s onwards. Her vast wealth, coupled with remarkable taste, resulted in one of the most important collections anywhere in the world.

The contents list is a roll-call of almost every noteworthy artist in the first half of the 20th century, from Picasso and Bracque to Kandinsky, Dalí, Miró, Magritte, Mondrian, de Chirico and Klee. Two artists she especially favoured were Max Ernst, who became her second husband, and Jackson Pollock, a Guggenheim discovery. If Pollock's random splatterings have hitherto left you unmoved, the complexity and careful craftsmanship of *Moon Woman* or *Alchemy* may change your mind. The charming garden, where Peggy lies buried next to some of her beloved poodles, contains sculptures by Henry Moore, and a wickedly eye-catching work by Marino Marini called *The Angel of the City* (1948). The airy terrace café is an attractive place for a light lunch or snack. Talks and temporary exhibitions take place regularly. Open Wed–Mon 10:00–18:00 (until 20:00 on Sat).

La Salute and the Southern Waterfront

Two quite unmistakeable monuments grace the tip of Dorsoduro: the Baroque church of **Santa Maria della Salute**, and the golden globe on the old **Customs House**. Views from, as well as of, this part of Venice are nothing short of spectacular. A promenade known as the **Zattere** runs along Dorsoduro's sunny southern side, a popular place to stroll enjoying the views towards Giudecca, and perhaps an ice cream at Nico's wonderful *gelateria*. Inland, the quiet neighbourhoods between the canal strips (once separate *insulae* – islands) each have their own character. **San Trovaso** is a typical example. The western esplanade is occupied by the commercial port (Stazione Marittima), and inaccessible to the general public.

Above: *The elaborate Baroque exterior of Santa Maria della Salute.*
Opposite: *Visitors view the avant-garde at the Peggy Guggenheim Collection.*

Santa Maria della Salute ***

All visitors see this flamboyant church, if only from a distance, and few leave Venice without at least one photograph of its giant white domes silhouetted against the sunset. In 1630, a terrible outbreak of plague hit the city, wiping out over a third of its population. Less than a month after its foundation piles were laid, the epidemic stopped, and the Senate kept its vow to dedicate the church to the Virgin in gratitude for her intervention. Our Lady of Good Health dominates the entrance to the Grand Canal in fine style. It occupied its architect Baldassare Longhena for most of his working life, and wasn't completed until five years after he died. After the flamboyance of the exterior with its scrolls and statuary, the interior seems rather bleak, its octagonal nave radiating chilly geometric spaces beneath the soaring cupola. The high altar is certainly dramatic, its sculptural centrepiece by Giusto Le Corte representing *The Queen of Heaven Expelling the Plague* (1670). Amid the swirling Baroque, a tranquil Byzantine icon glows. The best of La Salute's art is in the sacristy to the left, where several masterpieces by Titian, and Tintoretto's *Marriage at Cana* (1561) can be seen. Open daily 09:00–12:00 and 15:00–17:30.

Bridges to Health

Similar ceremonies are held annually at two Venetian churches to commemorate deliverance from the plague. The **Festa del Redentore** (Feast of the Redeemer) takes place at the Redentore church towards the end of July. On 21 November, the feast day of the **Madonna della Salute** is celebrated in Dorsoduro. Pontoon boat-bridges are formed across the Grand and Giudecca canals so that worshippers can cross to give thanks. Candles are lit in the churches, and firework displays light up the lagoon.

Above: *One of Venice's last remaining gondola boatyards in the San Trovaso district.*
Opposite: *San Barnaba's vegetable barge is a regular fixture near the Ponte dei Pugni.*

Dogana di Mare **

This striking vantage point at the eastern tip of Dorsoduro boasts superb views. The 17th-century Maritime Customs House, topped by a distinctive gold sphere supported by two bronze figures of Atlas, is crowned by a weathervane sporting the goddess of Fortune. Today, the deserted quaysides differ from the days when all merchant shipping entering Venice berthed here for inspection. Plans are afoot to use this building as an annexe for the Guggenheim.

Zattere *

Fringing the Giudecca Canal, this long promenade is a wonderful place to watch the world go by. Its name arises from the large wooden rafts (*zattere*) once used for loading and unloading cargo. Some of the old salt warehouses (*salone*) lining the quaysides now house restaurants or craft studios. A few churches lie scattered along the Zattere: halfway along is the Gesuati (not to be confused with the Gesuiti in the north of the city), built when the Jesuit Order was suppressed; nearby stands the deconsecrated Santa Maria della Visitazione. Both have fine painted ceilings. Note the lion's mouth (*bocca di leone*) to the right of the Visitation church, a rare surviving denunciation box used in Republican days to complain about the state of the streets.

San Trovaso *

A short stroll behind the waterfront, this church dates from 1590, and stands on a quiet shabby square facing a canal. Though not one of Venice's most important churches, San Trovaso contains some good things, including Giambono's *St Chrysogonus on Horseback* in the chapel to the left of the main altar and a couple of accomplished Tintorettos. The marble bas-reliefs on the south chapel's altar front are very early, from around 1470. Open Mon–Sat 08:00–11:00 and 15:00–18:00; Sun 08:30–12:00.

Squero di San Trovaso

Between the Zattere and the church of San Trovaso lies one of Venice's oldest working gondola boatyards (*squero*). It dates from the 17th century, and still makes and repairs gondolas by traditional methods, using timber from the Dolomite forests. The slightly alpine appearance of the buildings indicates the origin of its first owners, who hailed from the mountainous Cadore region. The boatyard is closed to the public, but you can often watch work going on from the opposite bank of the canal.

Western and Northern Dorsoduro

Northwest of the Ponte dell'Accademia lies an intricate patchwork of quiet canals and countless bridges. One of the city's last 'floating markets', a photogenic vegetable barge, moors near the Ponte dei Pugni on Rio di San Barnaba. Small shops and bars cater for locals, others have an eye to the increasing numbers of visitors and resident expatriates who stray into this characterful zone. Venice's university is based in the Santa Marta quarter to the far southwest of the *sestiere*, adding a transient zest to a mostly working-class neighbourhood. Student cafés enliven the two age-old squares of **Santa Margherita** and **San Barnaba**. Arty, alternative happenings take place in venues unpublicized by the tourist offices. Eagle-eyed visitors may even spot the odd small disco discreetly signalled in some unobtrusive location. Fine palazzi occupy the prime sites by the Grand Canal; elsewhere, dwellings are humbler.

Ca' Rezzonico **

Now housing the **Museo del Settecento Veneziano** (Museum of 18th-century Venice), this fine waterfront palace is another Baroque masterpiece by Baldassare Longhena, begun in 1667. Funds ran out halfway through its construction, and it was another century before the Rezzonicos, a wealthy merchant banking family, moved in to lead a sumptuous lifestyle of banquets and balls as the celebrity socialites of their day. A huge ballroom by Giorgio Massari takes pride of place among many lavishly decorated rooms on the *piano nobile*, with trompe l'œil frescoes, chinoiserie and gilded chandeliers. Elsewhere, Tiepolo ceilings, scenes by Guardi and Canaletto, and period furniture evoke a vivid picture of how the rich lived in 18th-century Venice. On the upper floor, an old pharmacy has been reconstructed from Campo San Stin. The palace is currently undergoing restoration, so future opening times are uncertain.

Palatial Ends

Two sumptuous palaces along north Dorsoduro's waterfront witnessed the death of their famous residents. The magnificent Gothic **Ca' Foscari** saw the sad demise of **Francesco Foscari**, one of the longest-serving Venetian doges. After 34 years in office he was harried into a decline by political enemies who falsely exiled his son for treason. The frail old man was forced to resign and died of depression soon afterwards. A few doors away, **Ca' Rezzonico** was the final home of the English poet **Robert Browning**, who bought the palace in partnership with his son Pen in 1888, and died here the following year of bronchitis.

San Pantalon *

Breathtaking ceiling paintings deck this externally unprepossessing church in the far north of Dorsoduro. Created on sixty panels by 17th-century artist Fumiani, this is allegedly the largest work of art on painted canvas in the world. The subject, as obscure as its creator, is *The Martyrdom and Glory of St Pantalon*, a physician credited with great healing powers. Sadly, just as Fumiani completed his epic 24-year project, he plunged from the scaffolding to his death. Open Sun–Fri 16:00–18:00.

Campo Santa Margherita **

This large sprawling square, peaceful but never dull, is the heart of community life in Dorsoduro. Market stalls sell fruit and fish in the mornings, and a tide of varied humanity – children, pensioners, visitors, students and locals – flows through to sample terrace cafés, or buy bread and groceries, herbal remedies and outré clothes. At night the bars entice a cool young crowd. Ancient buildings surround the square. The deconsecrated church at the north end is now a forum for university events (quaint façade carvings relate the startling tale of St Margaret, swallowed by an exploding dragon). Isolated by the fish stalls is the tiny Scuola dei Varotari, the ancient tanners' guildhall, sporting a blurry carving of its patron Madonna.

Opposite: *Watching the world go by with the pigeons in Campo Santa Margherita.*
Below: *A café scene on Campo Santa Margherita.*

Santa Maria dei Carmini *

The much-altered 14th-century church of the Carmelite Order makes a prominent statement slap in the middle of Dorsoduro. The richly decorated interior glows dimly with dark gilded statues and columns draped in crimson damask; nave and ceiling are smothered with sombre paintings. Further devotional works decorate the side-altars but need lighting up for the best effect: Cima de Conegliano's *Adoration of the Shepherds* (1509) is second on the right; Lorenzo Lotto's *St Nicolas of Bari with Saints* (1529) hangs in its opposite number on the left. The canopied side entrance porch has early carvings of animals and birds. In the nearby *scuola*, dating from 1663, Giambattista Tiepolo's ceiling paintings grace the upper hall. Use a mirror to prevent neck-ache. The church is open daily 07:30–12:00 and 14:30–19:10 (16:30 on Sun); the *scuola* is open Mon–Sat 09:00–18:00, Sun 09:00–16:00.

San Sebastiano ⋆

Veronese, one of the last great masters of the Venetian Renaissance, was commissioned to decorate this church during the 16th century. The sacristy, choir, nave and even the organ door panels, are smothered with opulent frescoes showing figures in the richly coloured costumes of Venice's heyday. Those on the nave ceiling relate the story of Esther, while the church's patron, San Sebastian, is depicted in the chancel. Paolo Veronese hailed, of course, from Verona, but Venice claims him as her own, and he is buried in this church, by the organ. Open Mon–Sat 10:00–17:00.

San Nicolò dei Mendicoli ⋆⋆

Tucked away in one of the most remote corners of the city, this little Medieval church is undeservedly neglected by most visitors. Its low-lying location in an old fishermen's quarter left it at constant risk of flooding for many years. Now reinforced against damp, and handsomely restored by the Venice in Peril conservation fund, it is well worth tracking down as one of the most charming and ancient of Venice's minor churches. Its interior is surprisingly sumptuous, the nave decked with gilded statues and the walls and ceiling covered with paintings by artists of the Veronese School. During Sunday services the church is bathed in golden candlelight and filled with flowers and music, a well-used communal place of worship. The exterior of the building has a 15th-century porch, one of only two extant examples in Venice, built to provide shelter for the poor. Open daily 10:00–12:00 and 16:00–18:00.

Bridge Battles

Several bridges in Venice, including the Ponte dei Pugni over the Rio di San Barnaba, are inset with white marble footprints at each corner. These mark the starting positions of ritualized fist-fights between the two rival Venetian clans, the Castellani and the Nicolotti. Hostilities generally took place during the autumn, the aim being to secure control of the bridge. The fights were extremely vicious, no-holds-barred affairs. Many combatants ended up in the canals, sometimes badly injured or even killed. Eventually these authorized punch-ups were banned, and Venice's competitive instincts were channelled in safer directions, such as boat races.

7
Lagoon Islands

From time to time, central Venice's tourist crowds and tightly packed buildings can seem oppressive. With so much to look at, sightseeing may easily become a burden instead of a pleasure. This is just the time to recharge your batteries by taking a boat trip across the lagoon to visit some of the 40 or so smaller islands. All can be reached within an hour. A dozen or so of the more interesting ones are on regular *vaporetto* or *motonave* routes. Others, privately owned or uninhabited, are accessible only by water-taxi or private launch. Setting off into this magical blue-green archipelago, preferably in the early morning, is an unforgettable adventure. Any of the major islands can provide a good fish lunch, but a lagoon outing is an ideal opportunity for a picnic. Don't forget your camera.

Top Attractions

*** **San Giorgio Maggiore:** Palladio's Benedictine church with the best *campanile* views in Venice.
*** **Torcello:** Byzantine mosaics and remarkable churches in Venice's ancient precursor far across the northern lagoon.
** **Murano:** the glass island, often unfairly dismissed as the preserve of tour groups on whistle-stop visits.
** **Burano:** the lace island, a postcard scene of gaily painted fishermen's cottages.
** **Giudecca:** visit the lovely Redentore Church.

Opposite: *The cathedral of Santa Maria dell'Assunta on Torcello.*

Boats pick their way carefully through this shallow jumble of half-hidden sandbanks and reed marshes – no mean feat with constantly changing water lines and sea fogs, despite the marked channels of *bricole* (bundled poles). The thin sandspits (*lidi*) which were formed by silt from the Po Delta give the lagoon some protection from Mediterranean storms, but cannot withstand the abnormal surge tides that occur with increasing frequency through the winter months. A controversial system of movable water gates, dubbed the *MOSE* project (*Modulo Sperimentale Elettromeccanico*), was recently constructed near the Lido in the hopes of preventing further disastrous floods like those of 1966 (*see* panel, page 16).

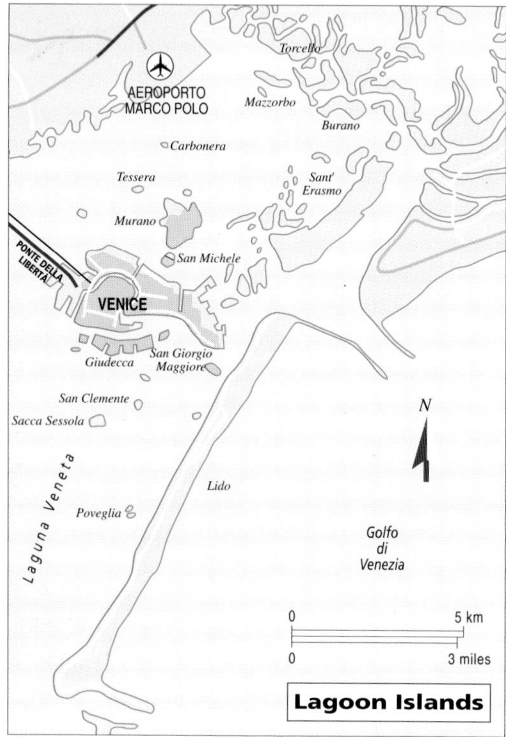

Many of the islands were inhabited in earlier centuries, and turned to a great variety of purposes: monasteries, isolation hospitals, mental asylums, burial grounds, pleasure gardens, gunpowder factories. More recent uses include craft workshops, art restoration centres, beach resorts, market gardens, fish farms and wildlife reserves.

Southern Islands

San Giorgio Maggiore ***

The tiny **monastery island** opposite the Piazzetta makes a theatrical focal point from St Mark's and the Riva degli Schiavoni. Mirrored in the waters of the lagoon, the magnificent **Benedictine complex** designed by Andrea Palladio is one of the city's most familiar monuments. It was built between 1559 and 1580, a harmonious neo-Classical amalgam which looks especially impressive bathed in morning or evening light. Lagoon views from the top of its campanile, reached by a lift, are probably the best in Venice. Immediately below lie the monastery cloisters, enclosing lawns like velvet carpets. These and the rest of the island belong to the Cini Foundation, and are accessible only for special cultural events. The church, rather austere inside, contains Jacopo Bassano's *Adoration of the Shepherds* (1582) and several important works by Tintoretto. *The Last Supper* and *The Fall of Manna* (both 1594) are in the chancel; *The Deposition* (1592–94) hangs in the Cappella della Morte. A

Opposite: *The Palladian monastery complex of San Giorgio Maggiore.*

dragon-slaying scene by Carpaccio can be visited in an upper room. Behind the high altar, the carved choir stalls deserve a look. Open daily 09:30–12:30, 14:30–18:30.

Cat-love… has happ… once vast p… and hungry … assured that t… …en no council-spor… …ed mass poisoning – they have simply been relocated to the island of San Clemente by an animal rights charity. Another island, Lazzaretto Vecchio near the Lido, is a home for stray dogs, though not nearly enough of them have been exiled here. The unwanted souvenirs that visitors find on their shoes are among the least agreeable features of strolling round central Venice.

Giudecca **

Also known as Spinalunga (which means 'long spine'), or the **Garden Isle**, Giudecca has undergone several changes through the centuries. Behind its northern waterfront promenade, it is now quiet and rather shabby, its alleys petering out in wasteland, its convents and palaces neglected. In Medieval times it was something of a place of exile and retreat, for troublesome aristocrats or Jews who were not permitted to live in the city centre. Later, in the days of the Republic, it was used as a summer resort where Venice's more privileged citizens built palatial villas and pleasure gardens. The 19th century saw the development of an industrial sector of breweries and factories. The abandoned **Mulino Stucky**, Venice's official flour mill, on its western side is one of Giudecca's most notable landmarks, currently scheduled for redevelopment as a hotel and apartment complex. The exclusive **Cipriani**, one of the world's most luxurious hotels, stands in a large secluded site at the eastern end of the island.

The long northern quayside promenade looks over towards Dorsoduro's Zattere and the church of Santa Maria della Salute. **Harry's Dolci** (an outpost of Harry's Bar in San Marco) makes a popular summer excursion destination (*see* Where to Eat, page 119). The main attraction on the island is the large church of **Il Redentore** (the Redeemer), built, like La Salute, in gratitude for deliverance from the terrible plague in 1576. Its restrained interior offers a typical Palladian lesson in Classical geometry. It also boasts an elegant altarpiece and several good paintings, some of which are tucked away in the sacristy (Alvise Vivarini's tranquil *Madonna and Child*, and a Veronese *Baptism*). Minor landmarks situated along the waterfront are Venice's handsome youth hostel, enjoying wonderful views, and the church of Le Zitelle, now used as a congress centre.

International Film Festival

Since 1932, a highlight of the Lido's hectic summer calendar has been this glamorous cinematic event, when celebrities gather on the promenades of the Lungomare Marconi to be lionized by fans and *paparazzi*. This is the oldest film festival in the world, set up for the Biennale exhibition and now staged annually in late August/early September. The Palazzo del Cinema, built in Fascist times, is the main venue for film shows; the stars tend to congregate by the terrace bars of the Excelsior Hotel.

Lido *

The slender sand strip separating the Venetian lagoon from the open sea has given its name to any number of **bathing places** worldwide. At 12km (8 miles) long, it is one of the largest islands in the archipelago. Visitors from central Venice generally take one of several frequent *vaporetto* routes to the Lido, landing in the

Below: *Italians flock to the Lido beaches all summer long. The sections nearest the luxury hotels are carefully looked after, but expensive.*

middle of its western side within about ten minutes. With motorized traffic, and scarcely any ancient buildings, it has a very different feel from the rest of the lagoon. Buses ply along the island's spinal roads from the ferry terminus, and bikes can be hired for exploring. Long beaches of shelly sand line its Adriatic coast, overlooking parades of passing shipping and backed by wooden bathing huts. Deserted and forlorn out of season, the beaches are neatly brushed and combed between June and September, each section parcelled into concessions of expensive sunbeds and parasols.

Tourism on the Lido first began in earnest in the 1850s, when sea bathing was all the rage. By the early 20th century, it had become one of the world's most glamorous resorts, full of fashionable Liberty (Art Nouveau) villas, palatial *belle époque* hotels, Venice's summer casino and a golf course. Residents live here all year round, but outside its short summer season the atmosphere is very different. Changing patterns of tourism and deteriorating water quality have made the Lido less popular in recent years. But the stately pleasure domes of the **Hotel Excelsior** and the **Hotel des**

Above: *The Cipriani Hotel's terrace restaurant occupies an enviable waterfront site.*

Poetic Water Babies

'... a bare strand
Of hillocks, heaped from ever-shifting sand,
Matted with thistles and amphibious weeds
... an uninhabited seaside ...'
(Shelley, *Julian and Maddalo*)

Long before the Lido became a fashionable resort, Shelley, Byron and other Grand Tour *literati* found it a tranquil retreat from the bustle of the city. Byron was a champion swimmer, the only finisher in an epic race from the Lido to the Rialto. Shelley was less lucky in the water, and died by drowning while sailing off the Tuscan coast in 1822.

Bains along the Lungomare Marconi still pack in some glitzy guests, especially when the International Film Festival is in full swing. Apart from the idiosyncratic hotels and villas, which display some inventive architectural flourishes, the Lido has few sights. The most interesting area lies to the north, where there is a **Jewish cemetery** and the church and monastery of **San Nicolò**, which the doge would visit each year after the Marriage to the Sea ceremony. Today, a flying club offers joyrides over the lagoon.

The Marriage to the Sea

This famous ceremony began around the year AD1000, when Venice gained control of the Dalmatian coast. It represented the city's inseparable relationship with the sea and in earlier times, its maritime supremacy. During the days of the Republic, the doge would ride in his golden barge, the *Bucintoro*, to the Lido, and drop a wedding ring into the sea with the words: 'We espouse thee, O Sea, in sign of our true and perpetual dominion over thee.' This was followed by a service in San Nicolò church, and revelling in St Mark's Square. Divers competed to recover the ring and, if successful, received a prize. Rival sea powers ridiculed the ceremony; one Ottoman Sultan predicted it wouldn't be long before the doge consummated his marriage by falling overboard.

Northern Islands

San Michele *

Clearly visible across the straits from Fondamente Nuove, the **'Island of the Dead'** casts a certain mournful fascination, and makes a surprisingly interesting place for a quiet, contemplative stroll. It lies on several regular boat routes. Gravelled paths separate the blocks of graves, shaded by stately cypress trees and flanked by tall curtain walls. Lizards, sea birds and the Franciscan monks who tend the graves add reassuring signs of life. Widows arrive with fresh bouquets, using the watering cans provided to top up the vases. San Michele was designated for its current purpose by Napoleonic decree, when Venice's overcrowded central cemeteries threatened public health. The simple 15th-century church of **San Michele in Ísola**, by the landing stage, is faced in white Istrian stone. Cemetery plans can be obtained from the reception office, pointing out celebrity graves, like those of **Ezra Pound** (1885–1972), **Sergei Diaghilev** (1872–1929) and **Igor Stravinsky** (1882–1971) which lie in the neglected Protestant section. Hundreds of humbler graves, lovingly decked with flowers, photographs and family testaments, are a more moving insight into the Venetian way of death. Slightly disquieting, though, is the discovery that after a decade or so, many remains are dug up and taken to yet another island, Sant'Ariano, to make room for new arrivals. Open Apr–Sept 07:30–18:00, Oct–Mar 07:30–16:00.

Murano **

The '**Island of Glass**' acquired its soubriquet in 1291, when the glass-makers and their furnaces were moved here to reduce the danger of fire in the centre of the city. This was the beginning of a period of great prosperity. The glass-blowers enjoyed special privileges, though they were forbidden on pain of death to take their trade secrets outside the confines of the Republic. Murano had been settled since the 5th century, and soon became a flourishing Adriatic trading centre. It enjoyed some autonomy from Venice, employing its own police force, and minting its own coins.

Today, Murano is a major excursion destination. A large number of visitors see it on various organized tours, which include obligatory visits to glass-blowing demonstrations and showrooms (often at ludicrously high speed). It is very easy to arrange a trip independently, with no pressure to buy anything and a chance to enjoy a leisurely wander round the quietly dignified, workmanlike streets away from the more commercialized areas. Several age-blackened palaces survive along the waterside *fondamente*, dotted between dozens of glass studios (*fornaci*).

Often dismissed as vulgar tourist kitsch, Murano's glassware is in fact enormously varied. There is plenty of hideous, mass-produced stuff on

Hotel des Bains

The Hotel des Bains trades on its fame as the setting for Thomas Mann's novel *Death in Venice*, widely popularized by Luchino Visconti's 1971 film, starring Dirk Bogarde. It evokes the decadent atmosphere of the Lido in its *belle époque* heyday, when royalty mingled with plutocrats and socialites in the deckchairs and striped *cabanas* by these grand hotels, while the storm clouds of war and cholera gathered overhead. Today, the Hotel des Bains is still an elegant and expensive, if suitably melancholic, place to stay.

Opposite: *Tightly packed graves on the cemetery island of San Michele.*
Below: *A glass-blower demonstrates his skills in a factory in Murano.*

...it
...e
...oison
... But it could
...ealer too.
Ra... slivers of glass,
embedded in a metal haft,
made an unpleasant weapon for the notorious secret police employed by the Council of Ten in late Medieval times. When sunk into a victim's flesh, the glass blade would snap, leaving a virtually undetectable wound to fester agonizingly.

sale, some of it in fact imported from the Far East rather than made locally. But just a short walk along the quaysides of the main canals will take you past some truly elegant shops selling attractive jewellery, designer lamps and vases, and flamboyant Murano chandeliers. Several of the most prestigious producers have retail outlets in central Venice (*see* Shopping, page 121).

For an interesting perspective on the glass-making industry, visit the **Museo Vetrario**, which is grandly housed in the Palazzo Giustiniani, a former residence of the Bishop of Torcello. The building itself is well worth a look in its own right. The well-displayed contents of the museum include more than 4000 pieces of glassware, ranging from early grave goods in pallid, aqueous shades to handsome modern pieces in vivid, rainbow colours. There are scent jars, flagons and goblets, false gems (a brisk trade in Renaissance Venice) an ambitious table centrepiece of an Italian garden, and the famous enamelled Barovier Cup (a 15th-century wedding gift) in rich deep blue. The museum is open Thu–Tue 10:00–17:00.

Below: *The apse of Santi Maria e Donato, a harmonious example of Venetian Romanesque style.*

Close to the Glass Museum is Murano's other major sight, the 12th-century basilica of **Santi Maria e Donato**, one of the oldest in the lagoon. The apse end, which faces the canal, is particularly eye-catching, in mellow brown brick with Romanesque blind arcading and dog's-tooth chevrons. Inside, the floor is a colourful jigsaw of geometric and allegorical designs, and the focal point is a lovely apsidal mosaic of the Madonna done in blue on a golden background. Look out for the 'dragon bones' slung behind the altar, reputedly killed by St Donatus (who spat at it). The basilica is open daily, 08:00–12:00 and 16:00–19:00. A second church, **San Pietro Martire**, situated on the Fondamenta dei Vetrai, contains a couple of Bellinis and a Veronese, and is lit by ornate Murano chandeliers.

Burano **

This blithe little island is much loved for its prettily painted houses, all the colours of Italian ice cream, which make a picturesque scene reflected in its canals. You will probably find a quayside artist or two recording views of boats and bridges against this kaleidoscopic backdrop. Few of its buildings have great architectural pretensions, but they seem very neat, even when draped with washing, after the eroded, peeling façades of many Venetian buildings. The church of **San Martino** contains a *Crucifixion* by Tiepolo (being restored), but perhaps more memorable than its calm, fragrant interior is its alarmingly skewed campanile, one of Venice's most dramatic leaning towers.

Above: *Colourful canal-side houses on the island of Burano.*

Burano now has around 4000 inhabitants, who traditionally earn their living from **fishing** and **lace**. The products of both industries are much in evidence on the main street of Via Baldassare Galuppi (named after an 18th-century Buranese composer). Tasty ways of preparing lagoon fish can be found on local menus. Burano's most distinctive product is lace, refined on this island from a mere social accomplishment to an exquisite art form. The mysteries of *punto in aria*, *controtagliato*, and *punto de Venezia* can be discovered in the **Museo del Merletto**, where there is also a school of lace-making, in a Gothic palazzo on the main square. The antique pieces on display here are dazzling and intricate. An altar cloth called the *Mysteries of the Rosary* contains a series of complex biblical scenes all executed in minute lace loops. Teaching boards show enlarged versions of the traditional Buranese stitches, which are often too microscopic to see with the naked eye. Open Wed–Mon 10:00–17:00.

Burano's Houses

'In the middle of it there bursts a sudden splurge of rather childish colour, its reflections spilling into the water, and staining these lugubrious channels like an overturned paint-pot … Its campanile leans at a comical angle, and it is packed tightly with hundreds of bright little houses, like a vivid adobe village in a dismal desert: red and blue houses, yellow and orange and blazing white, a jumble of primary colours shining in the mud.' (Jan Morris, Venice 1960)

Above: *The bell tower of Torcello's cathedral makes a useful landmark.*

In its heyday, lace made a great contribution to the Venetian economy, and was exported throughout Europe. Foreign competition caused a sharp decline during the 19th century, and fearing that the skills would be lost, a school was established to preserve the tradition.

Torcello ***

If you have time for only one lagoon excursion, make it Torcello. The ghosts of this melancholy island with its exquisite **cathedral** will haunt you long after you have left. Torcello was probably the first area of the Venetian lagoon to be colonized during the 5th and 6th centuries, and it rapidly grew into a thriving settlement with a population of perhaps 20,000, trading in wool and salt. But twin disasters struck. Its canals silted, and malaria spread insidiously through its marshy terrain until it became uninhabitable. Eventually its citizens abandoned it, fleeing to other Venetian islands. Plundered for building materials, all that remains of its glorious past is a cluster of historic monuments with a museum, a few restaurants and souvenir stalls, and silent sluggish canals. The rest of the island is a green expanse of fields and salt marshes, where ducks, herons and white egrets search for frogs and fish among sea lavender and tamarisk trees. Today, its resident population numbers just a few dozen.

Torcello is reached as a side-trip from Burano (check the boat routes, which are complicated). From the landing stage, follow the canal path past the unparapeted Devil's Bridge (**Ponte del Diavolo**) and the island's three restaurants. The beckoning finger ahead is the tall campanile of **Santa Maria dell'Assunta**, Venice's first cathedral, founded in AD639. Next to it is the serenely porticoed church of **Santa Fosca**, one of the most architecturally satisfying anywhere in Venice, a blend of east and west in elegant geometry. It dates from around 1100, and its simple Greek-cross Byzantine interior makes a dignified setting for the relics of its martyred patron which rest beneath the altar. Open daily 10:00–12:30, 14:00–17:00.

LACE-MAKING

Legend has it that a sailor was given a piece of intricate seaweed by a mermaid, and brought it home to his beloved as a bridal veil. The girl replicated the seaweed patterns with her needle, and so the art of lace-making was born. Buranese lace is noted for its delicacy, and is made like embroidery with needle and thread rather than with bobbins. Stitched to a parchment backing which is then removed, the lace patterns remain unsupported as if by magic (*punti in aria* – points in air). Seven different stitches can be found in traditional Burano lace. A team of workers each specialize in a single stitch, passing the lace from hand to hand. *Roselline* are little star-shapes; *contro-tagliato* are large scrolls; *punto de Venezia* has bar patterns, alleged to represent the bridges of Venice.

Torcello's main attraction, however, is the **Veneto-Byzantine cathedral**, where there is much to see (collect the well-produced audioguide included in the entrance charge). The focal point in its simple, charming interior is the beautiful apse mosaic, a 12th-century *Mater Dolorosa* showing the Madonna holding the infant Christ; the handkerchief prefigures unshed tears. The frieze beneath it shows the twelve apostles. Other outstanding mosaics decorate the floor and side-chapels, but the most startling cover the rear wall, a graphic six-tier *Last Judgement*. Christ in Glory and his jewelled angels welcome the elect from their tombs, while those found wanting in the scales of judgement are cast into everlasting punishment amid flames and blue demons. Serpents spring through the eye-sockets of skulls, and gluttons chew off their own hands. Other interesting features include the marble panels of the iconostasis (rood screen), superbly carved with peacocks, and the waterlogged crypt. The bell tower can be climbed for an extensive view of the island and lagoon. Open daily 10:30–17.30.

The grassy piazza outside the cathedral contains a random assortment of archaeological fragments, including the quaint 5th-century **Attilla's Throne**. Here the **Museo dell'Estuario** occupies two small palaces; a few diverting objects lurk among a miscellany of axe heads, seals, bronzes, pottery and carvings from around the lagoon. Open Tue–Sun 10:00–12:30, 14:00–17:30 (16:00 Oct–Mar; lunchtime opening depends on volunteer staff).

MINOR ISLANDS

San Francesco del Deserto: a tiny green oasis, home to a small monastic community. The lovely gardens contain a tree said to have sprouted from the staff of St Francis.
San Lazzaro degli Armeni: a former leper colony, now an Armenian monastic complex. Lord Byron worked here on an Armenian–English dictionary.
San Giacomo in Paludo: a new conservation project includes a European Centre for the Environment.
San Servolo: variously used as a monastery, a hospital and an asylum; now contains centres for art restoration, international study and cancer research.
Poveglia: once an isolation ward for plague victims and later an old people's home, it now has market gardens and vineyards, with plans for a youth tourism centre.
Sacca Sessola: an artificial island created from lagoon dredgings, with a TB sanatorium until 1980. The dangerous straits nearby were the scene of sinister drownings ordered by the Council of Ten.

Left: *The graceful exterior of Santa Fosca, next to the cathedral in Torcello.*

8
Excursions from Venice

Most visitors find plenty to do within the confines of the Venetian lagoon, but the Veneto region offers much more. Ancient Roman frontier posts like **Verona**, **Vicenza**, **Padua** and **Treviso**, all even older than Venice itself, bristle with historic monuments and works of art, yet have an economic dynamism and a sense of style that propel them to the forefront of modern Italian culture. Landscapes encompass spectacular alpine wilderness areas, where natural grandeur challenges the man-made splendours of the towns and cities. The **Dolomites**, rising to altitudes of over 2000m (6500ft), and the beautiful **Lago di Garda** present superb recreational facilities all year round. The main historic centres are easy to reach and explore in a day trip by efficient bus and train services from Venice. For lengthier tours of the mountains, or flexible pottering through the idyllic foothills, it is more convenient to hire a car from Piazzale Roma.

During the early centuries of the Republic, attention focused on expanding and defending Venice's maritime interests in the Adriatic, but by the Renaissance, La Serenissima realized that its own hinterland posed the biggest threat to its security. In the 15th century, Venice began to extend its control from the Veneto towards the Dolomites. Political confidence and economic prosperity fostered a surge of artistic creativity. The glories of ancient Greece and Rome were revived in countless variations on Classical themes. One of the most influential figures of the age was **Andrea Palladio**, a Paduan architect who began his career as a humble stonecutter in Vicenza.

Don't Miss

*** **Padua:** Giotto's fresco cycle in the Scrovegni Chapel is just one drawcard.
*** **Verona:** highlights are a monumental Roman amphitheatre and a spectacular Romanesque church.
*** **Vicenza:** Palladio's elegant showcase; the Villa Rotonda has inspired imitations worldwide.
*** **The Dolomites:** an outdoor paradise in dramatic saw-toothed mountains.
*** **Lake Garda:** the biggest of the northern lakes.

Opposite: *Lake Garda is a paradise for watersports enthusiasts.*

St Anthony of Padua

Padua's patron saint (1195–1231) was a Portuguese missionary who joined the Franciscan order after surviving a shipwreck. Like St Francis (whom he probably knew), Anthony's life was a model of kindness, humility and devotion to the poor. He preached in Bologna as well as Padua, and was known for his fine sermons. His help is invoked for many reasons, one being to find lost property!

Brenta Villas

One of the main routes inland from Venice is the valley of the River Brenta, canalized in the 16th century as far as Padua. Wealthy Venetians began to buy land on either side of this strategic waterway, partly to grow crops and raise livestock, but also as rural retreats from city life. The placid surroundings and clean air made a much more appealing environment for the stifling summer months, and the Brenta Riviera soon turned into a fashionable resort. Country villas sprang up along the banks, and the celebrity architects and artists of the day were kept busy as aristocratic patrons competed to outdo each other by commissioning ever more refined and splendid homes.

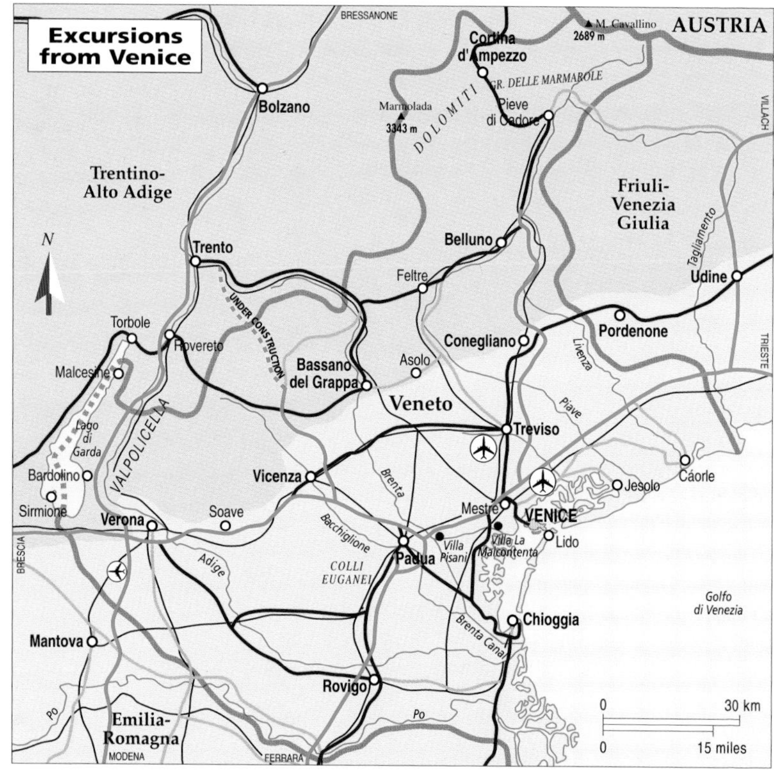

Of the 80 or so Renaissance villas between Malcontenta and Stra, about 10 are now open to the public. Several can easily be reached on scheduled bus routes from Venice, or organized tours. One of the most spectacular is **Villa Pisani**, a vast 18th-century pile, situated just outside Padua, built for a wealthy banking family. Though stripped of its original furnishings by Napoleon, frescos by Giambattista Tiepolo and his son Giandomenico survive inside. Rear views overlook an impressive formal garden with a topiary maze and a long ornamental lake. At the Venetian end of the Brenta Canal stands the much older **Villa Foscari**, popularly known as **La Malcontenta**, an interesting example of Palladio's work, designed in 1559 with forceful Roman features. The viewing rooms off the central hallway are covered in frescos.

Above: *Classical figures decorate the entrance façade of the Villa Pisani near Padua, one of the most impressive Brenta villas open to the public.*

PADUA

Only half an hour's journey west by road or rail, Padua is Venice's nearest major city – an ideal day trip. Its strategic location and communication links made it an attractive settlement site even in prehistoric times; Padua can claim with some justification to be the cradle of Veneto civilization. Under imperial rule, its prosperity was second only to Rome's. Still an affluent place with a long academic tradition dating from 1222, its university students play an important role in city life, and its year-round programme of cultural events. Luckily, most of its Medieval buildings escaped air-raid damage during World War II. Weekday street markets selling fruit and vegetables add colour to the squares around its ancient court of justice, the **Palazzo della Ragione**. Wine bars, restaurants and speciality shops shelter in its colonnaded buildings. An old-fashioned coffee house, the Classical-looking **Caffè Pedrocchi**, has been a meeting place for intellectuals since the early 19th century. The huge **Prato della Valle** is an oval piazza of water gardens and statues, site of a former Roman theatre.

THE *BURCHIELLO*

Leisurely if expensive boat trips between Venice and Padua revive a tradition established in the 18th century, when Grand Tour visitors chartered a barge called the *Burchiello* to sail along the Brenta Canal, stopping at some of these palatial houses. In those days, a few coins proffered to one of the household staff would ensure admission; the access arrangements are now more formalized. Today's equivalent motor-launch sets off on alternate days from Venice or Padua between March and November, stopping to see several villas and have lunch en route. Return trips are made by rail or bus. Tickets are available from many travel agents in Venice.

Above: *Statuary depicting eminent citizens surrounds the ornamental canal of Padua's Prato della Valle.*

Padua's two greatest sights are the **Cappella degli Scrovegni**, containing one of Italy's most important fresco cycles, and the **Basilica di Sant' Antonio**, dubbed simply **Il Santo**, a Byzantine treasure house dedicated to Padua's sweet-natured patron saint. Padua's sightseeing potential is not exhausted after visiting these buildings: palaces, museums, churches, Roman remains, botanic gardens and its ancient university are also worth exploring.

Cappella degli Scrovegni ***

The wall-paintings in this small chapel constitute a turning point in European art. Built by a Paduan nobleman, Enrico Scrovegni, to atone for the supposed sins of his usurious father, whom Dante condemned to eternal punishment in *The Inferno*, the chapel dates from 1303. For the next two years, the great Florentine artist Giotto worked on this ambitious fresco cycle showing scenes from the life of Christ. The naturalism and narrative drive of these 38 works mark a clear departure from the iconic, emblematic quality of Byzantine art, and a quantum shift towards the modern era. The starry barrel-vaulted ceiling infuses the entire chapel with a sapphire tinge; within each separate painting, figures in jewel-coloured robes enact their biblical drama against complex architectural perspectives and detailed Renaissance landscapes. The west wall, in a slightly more primitive style, depicts the *Last Judgement*.

Just outside the Scrovegni Chapel are the remains of a Roman amphitheatre. Housed in the neighbouring cloisters of a Medieval church are the **Musei Civici Eremitani**, Padua's civic museums, which consist of an art gallery (Veneto paintings), a coin-and-medal collection, and an archaeology section. The chapel and museums are open Tue–Sun 09:00–18:00 (combined ticket).

Botanic Garden

Padua's charming botanic garden (*Orto Botanico*) makes a tranquil change of scenery if you tire of buildings and bustle. Dating from 1545, it is the oldest in Europe, and retains much the same plan as it did when it was first constructed. One of its palm trees was allegedly planted in 1585. Medicinal plants take up many of its carefully organized beds, and its paths are shaded by venerable specimen trees. The 16th-century hothouses were used to cultivate exotic new imports like lilacs, sunflowers and potatoes.

Basilica di Sant'Antonio ***

This elaborate structure combines elements of Byzantine, Romanesque and Gothic architecture in its multi-domed exterior. The most significant feature inside is the Cappella dell'Arca, containing the shrine of St Anthony in the north transept, decked with votive offerings in thanks for the saint's intervention in car accidents, dread diseases and other misfortunes. Marble reliefs depicting St Anthony's life decorate the shrine and the high altar, by the renowned sculptors Sansovino, Lombardo and Donatello. Other works of note include sculptures and a *Crucifixion* fresco by Altichiero da Zevio, enlivened with Medieval scenes. Open daily Oct–Mar 06:30–19:45, Nov–Feb 06:30–19:00.

VICENZA

Some 50km (30 miles) west of Venice on the Bacchiglione River, Vicenza is one of the wealthiest cities in Italy. Textiles and electronics are two contributors to its economic success. Most of its sights are within walking distance of its central square, the **Piazza dei Signori**, site of the massive so-called '**Basilica**', the first of Palladio's many projects in Vicenza. Also in this square stand the pencil-slim **Torre di Piazza** – an 82m (269ft) campanile from the 12th century – and the arcaded **Loggia del Capitaniato**, a former residence of the Venetian governor, now used for council meetings. Next to this is an elegant coffee house, the **Gran Caffè Garibaldi**. The main street (**Corso Palladio**) neatly bisects the historic quarter with a cross-section of Vicenzan features. Palladian palaces such as Palazzo Bonin (No. 13), Palazzo Zilere dal Verme (No. 42) and Palazzo da Schio (No. 147) intersperse shops and cafés tucked beneath the arcades. Best-known is the **Palazzo Valmarana**, dating from 1566 but not completed until a century after the architect's death. More examples of his work can be seen on the side-street called Contra Porti, along with some earlier Gothic palazzi in the Venetian style. Just outside the city is the **Villa Rotonda**, the most famously imitated of all Palladio's buildings.

PALLADIO'S DEBUT

The handsome Classical arcades of this imposing copper-roofed building on Piazza dei Signori encase, not a church or cathedral, but a 15th-century palace used as a town hall, which had become dangerously unstable. Palladio's first public project effectively buttressed the old Palazzo della Ragione in 1549, and cemented his own reputation. A marble statue in the square, often surrounded by market stalls, immortalizes the distinguished architect who did so much to give Vicenza a place in history. In fact, the city was rather unappreciative of him during his lifetime. Many of his designs were rejected, and he never won a single private commission here.

Below: *The Palladian Villa Rotonda, near Vicenza, has inspired grand civic architecture all over the world.*

Teatro Olimpico

This is Europe's oldest surviving indoor theatre, which Palladio began in 1579. He died before completing it, but his pupil, Vincenzo Scamozzi, continued his work. On its opening night, 3 March 1585, Sophocles' tragedy *Oedipus Rex* was performed. An adaptation of Hellenistic and Roman Classical amphitheatres, the auditorium consists of semi-circular tiered wooden benches below a balustrade of statues. A permanent stage-set using false perspectives and trompe l'œil creates an illusion of depth. Open same times as Museo Civico (combined ticket).

Not all Vicenza's historic buildings are Palladian. **Santa Corona** is a fine 13th-century church containing paintings by Giovanni Bellini and Paolo Veronese. **San Lorenzo** has a superbly carved Gothic doorway and serene cloisters. Even earlier is **Santi Felice e Fortunato**, Vicenza's oldest church, where 4th-century mosaics and a martyr's shrine have been excavated. **Casa Pigafetta**, situated near the River Retrone, is a lovely Spanish Gothic palazzo dating from 1481. Its owner, Antonio Pigafetta, was one of the few survivors of Magellan's round-the-world voyage in 1519–22.

Museo Civico **

Both the setting and the contents of Vicenza's civic museum are impressive. The **Palazzo Chiericati**, one of Palladio's best town houses, was built in 1550. Archaeological exhibits are displayed in the lavishly frescoed ground floor. Upstairs is a picture gallery with Gothic altarpieces from several local churches. Hans Memling's *Crucifixion* (1468–70) and Bartolomeo Montagna's Madonnas are especially fine. Open Tue–Sun, Apr–Sep 10:00–19:00, Oct–Mar 09:00–17:00.

Below: *Verona's Piazza delle Erbe has hosted a market for centuries.*

La Rotonda ***

The doll's-house perfection of this dazzling little villa built between 1550 and 1552 clinched Palladio's reputation as the most influential architect of all time. It was designed as a pleasure pavilion for a nobleman, Giulio Capra. Deceptively simple in concept – a shallow dome above a cube, each side sporting an identical six-columned, temple-like portico – its symmetrical proportions have inspired facsimiles from London to Delhi. It narrowly missed being selected as the prototype for Washington's White House. Open (gardens) Tue–Thu, Mar–Nov 10:00–12:00, 15:00–18:00; (interior) same hours, Wed only.

Verona

Verona is perhaps the Veneto's most enjoyable *città d'arte* (art city) – it is prosperous, stylish, and crammed with architectural monuments and works of art. Second only to Venice in size, this important centre became effectively the mainland capital of La Serenissima's empire. Verona is perhaps best known as the setting of Shakespeare's *Two Gentlemen of Verona*, and even more famously, *Romeo and Juliet*. Its other claim to fame is its superb Roman **amphitheatre** now used as the venue for a celebrated summer opera festival.

Above: *The Arena, Verona – these days a venue for operatic entertainment rather than gladiatorial contests or public executions.*

Settlement in Verona predated the Romans, but it was under Roman rule that it first achieved real significance. The grid-like historic quarter is still laid out much as it was in the days of Emperor Augustus. Within its 16th-century walls, ancient palazzi studded with Roman marble rub shoulders with boutiques. Verona is anything but fossilized. Its main square, the **Piazza delle Erbe**, is one of the most beautiful of any Italian town, surrounded by restaurants, cafés and bars. The colourful produce market keeps up the traditions of the old Roman forum once sited here.

Verona's Churches

Verona has an exceptional number of fine churches (combined ticket available). Its **Duomo**, magnificent inside and out, boasts an *Assumption* by Titian, and Romanesque cloisters. Others to look out for are the handsomely frescoed **Sant'Anastasia** by the waterfront, ancient **Santo Stefano**, the domed **San Giorgio in Braida** with Veronese's *Martyrdom of St George*, and the tiny church of **Santa Maria Antica** containing the splendid Scaligeri tombs. Best of all, though, is the 12th-century **San Zeno Maggiore**, one of Italy's most ornate Romanesque churches. A ship's-keel ceiling, a Mantegna altarpiece, and superb bronze door panels are just some of its glories.

The Arena ***

Verona's oval amphitheatre is a remarkable survival from the ancient world. Its longest axis measures 139m (456ft), making it the third largest of its kind after Rome's Colosseum and a similar monument near Naples. The original structure could hold some 14,000 spectators – enough seating for virtually the city's entire population when it was first built in about AD30. Forty-four tiers of stone seats rise vertiginously from the central stage, where gladiators and wild beasts emerged from underground passages to tear each other to pieces for the diversion of onlookers. The word 'arena' refers to the sand that was scattered and raked between contests

Above: *A modern Juliet on the balcony of Verona's Casa di Giulietta.*

to soak up the gore. These bloody traditions continued even after the Romans had vanished, with public executions, bullfighting and bear-baiting staged in Medieval times. Nowadays the Arena plays host to rock concerts, theatre performances and its famous opera festival, which draws in capacity crowds during July and August. Savagery is mostly confined to the review columns. Open Tue–Sun 08:00–19:00 (08:15–15:00 in the opera season).

Castelvecchio ***

The elegant fortress built by Verona's Medieval rulers, the powerful Scaligeri family, has been tastefully converted into one of the Veneto's finest art galleries, the **Museo Civico d'Arte**. Built by Cangrande II in the mid-14th century, the castle is as interesting as the contents, and aerial walkways along its fish-tailed battlements give fine views of the city and surrounding countryside. Exhibits span several centuries, from late Roman to early Renaissance, featuring silver, jewellery, sculpture and weaponry as well as paintings. Its catalogue of Veneto celebrities includes Mantegna, Bellini, Veronese, Titian, Tintoretto and Tiepolo, though some of the works by anonymous Medieval artists are just as enjoyable. The castle is open Tue–Sun 09:00–18–30.

Casa di Giulietta **

The romantic legend of Romeo and Juliet is entirely fictional, but the star-crossed lovers' firm hold on the imagination of Verona's visitors is quite unshakeable. This quaint 13th-century inn (at No. 27 Via Cappello) with the balcony and the courtyard fits the role of 'Juliet's House' very well. Open Tue–Sun 08:00–19:00. The equally bogus 'Casa di Romeo' (a Gothic building in Via delle Arche Scaligeri) and 'Juliet's Tomb' (an empty sarcophagus in an old crypt) are nearby. Thousands of visitors obligingly suspend disbelief to troop round these fanciful settings.

Romeo and Juliet

Verona's tourist authorities make much of the city's associations with the romantic legend originally written by Luigi da Porto of Vicenza during the 1520s. The tale has spawned adaptations in many different art forms. Two noble families called the Capuleti and the Montecchi (the Montagues and Capulets of Shakespeare's play) did indeed exist, with castles just outside Vicenza, but there is no evidence that they were enemies. In Venice, however, the rival clans of the Castellani and the Nicolotti were literally at daggers drawn, settling their differences with vicious fights on the city's bridges (*see* panel, page 89).

Lakes and Mountains

Treviso *

This attractive old town lies less than half an hour away from Venice, close enough for one airline to offer Treviso Airport as a convenient alternative to Venice's main international airport, Marco Polo. If central Venice seems too crowded or expensive, the quiet canals of Medieval Treviso, flanked by frescoed, arcaded houses and shady willow trees, may provide the answer. It also makes an appealing stopover en route to the Dolomites. The main thoroughfare of **Calmaggiore** runs through the old quarter past the town hall, in the historic **Palazzo dei Trecento**. The **Duomo** (cathedral), altered several times since its 12th-century foundation, contains Titian's *Annunciation*, Pordenone's eyecatching *Adoration of the Shepherds*, and a monument for Bishop Zanetti by the Lombardo family. There are more notable works of art in the **Museo Civico**, including Lotto's *Portrait of a Dominican*, and in the frescoed church of **San Nicolò**.

The Scaligeri

During the turbulent Middle Ages, rival dynasties emerged as wealthy leaders struggled for military control of Italy's foremost cities. The Scaligeri family held sway around Verona and Lake Garda during the 13th and 14th centuries. Their rise to power was ruthless and their rule autocratic, but once established, they prevailed over a peaceful and cultivated society and became keen patrons of the arts. Their great castles in Sirmione and Verona survive as monuments to their 127-year rule.

Asolo *

Robert Browning and the exiled Queen of Cyprus, Caterina Cornaro, were just two of many notable visitors who spent pleasurable stays in this alluring little walled town among the buckled Dolomite foothills. These days you can do so in style at the Villa Cipriani, one of Italy's most prestigious hotels. Above the town, a Medieval fortress on Roman foundations (**La Rocca**) gives great views of vines, orchards and cypress-clad hillsides all around. Not for nothing is Asolo known as *la città dei cento orizzonti* ('the town with a hundred horizons'). One good reason to visit Asolo is to see the **Villa Barbaro** at Maser, 7km (4 miles) east, one of the most important country houses in the Veneto. This magnificent example of Palladio's work is decorated with wonderful frescos by Paolo Veronese. **Possagno**, 10km (6 miles) north, was the birthplace, family home and burial site of the sculptor Antonio Canova.

Below: *Sirmione's grand Rocca Scaligeri fortress makes a picturesque waterfront scene.*

LUCIANO BENETTON

The town of Treviso is not entirely antique, and keen followers of fashion know it as the headquarters of the trendsetting Benetton empire. This phenomenally successful Italian clothing chain now owns around 7000 retail outlets in 120 different countries. Largest of all is the one at London's Oxford Circus. Controversial advertising campaigns and high-profile political stances have kept the company in the headlines in recent years. Extensive sports interests include basketball and Formula One racing teams, the Nordica brand of ski boots, Prince tennis racquets, and one of Europe's most exclusive golf clubs at Asolo. And it all started when Lucky Luciano (group chairman and former Italian senator) sold his beloved accordion to buy his sister a knitting machine – or so the story goes!

Lago di Garda **

Lake Garda is Italy's largest lake, 52km (32 miles) long and over 16km (10 miles) wide at its broad southerly end. The femur-shaped body of water is large enough to create an exceptionally mild microclimate around its shores, which luxuriate in Mediterranean-style gardens with palms, olives and exotic flowering shrubs. This huge natural playground is a mecca for **outdoor pursuits** of all kinds, from tennis, cycling or horse-riding to many different water sports. Major international sailing events are held here. Diesel-powered 'steamers' ply around the lakeshore towns all through the summer, as well as faster hydrofoil ferries and catamaran excursion boats. An easy journey by car or public transport from Venice, Lake Garda features on dozens of organized excursions too. It is especially popular with German visitors; German is very much the second language of choice in all its resorts.

The lake narrows from its sunny southern end towards dramatic steep-sided cliffs. Luxury hotels stud the perimeter road called **La Gardesana**, which closely follows the waterfront, sometimes boring through rock tunnels, sometimes snaking along corniche ledges with panoramic views. Pastel-coloured settlements stud the shoreline. One eternally popular destination is **Sirmione**, which occupies a narrow peninsula at the southern end of the lake, dangling from the mainland by a bridge. This picturesque, traffic-free old town is guarded by a cleverly designed moated castle, where waterborne invaders could be trapped. The Roman poet Catullus owned a villa nearby; ruinous vestiges of villas and baths dating from the 1st century BC can be traced among ancient olive groves in the Grotte di Catullo. **Bardolino** is well known for its red wine, while the fishing village of **Torbole** has smart shops, good restaurants and sailing events. From **Malcesine**, cable cars ascend the summit of Monte Baldo, a limestone ridge above the eastern shores.

Below: *Torbole on Lake Garda is a leading resort for windsurfing.*

Dolomites ***

These mountains offer some of the best, most extensive ski runs in the Alps. Italy's foremost winter sports resorts are here: **Cortina d'Ampezzo**, **Arabba** and **Madonna di Campiglio** attract a jetset crowd to the huge snowfields of the Selva and the Sella Ronda. The highest peak is the **Marmolada** at 3343m (10,968ft), glaciated all year round. On a clear day, the summits of the northern Veneto can be seen from central Venice. It is hard to imagine a greater scenic contrast between this fever-chart topography and the low-lying, pancake-flat coastline. When the lower slopes burst into flower-filled meadows at snowmelt, the ski-lifts and cable cars crank into action once again so that hikers and climbers can enjoy this majestic area. Much of the terrain, with hidden villages in steep-sided valleys, is accessible only with boots or skis, via waymarked trails studded with mountain refuge huts. But motorists can get some idea of these glaciated landforms of fossilized coral by following the spectacular **Strada delle Dolomiti** (Dolomite Road) from Bolzano to Cortina d'Ampezzo.

The Dolomites take their name from the renowned French geologist Deodat Dolomieu (1750–1801), though like Lake Garda the region has a strong Germanic flavour. Historically, it was part of the Austro-Hungarian Empire until 1918, and its strategic passes saw some of the Great War's bitterest mountain campaigns. The typical Tyrolean architecture of onion-domed churches and wide-eaved chalets brimming with geraniums is a clear legacy of Habsburg rule. **Belluno**, in a picturesque setting on the southern flanks of the Dolomites, is one of the largest and most interesting of the mountain towns. The densely forested **Cadore** region towards the eastern side of the range once supplied Venice with construction timber for its warships, gondolas, and the millions of foundation poles which shore up its buildings. Titian grew up in a small cottage at Pieve di Cadore.

Above: *The mountain scenery around Cortina d'Ampezzo attracts visitors all year round.*

Overleaf: *A twilight view of Verona, overlooking the Roman Ponte Pietra.*

Dolomite Wildlife

After central Venice, where pigeons, sparrows, gulls and a few mosquitoes comprise the wildlife you are likely to encounter, the biodiversity in the Dolomites is a revelation. Take binoculars and identification guides if you enjoy bird watching or plant hunting. Gentians, edelweiss and mountain lilies are typical summer flora. Golden eagles and griffon vultures soar over the highest crags, while ptarmigan camouflage themselves with a seasonal change of plumage. Roe deer are a common sight on the conifer-clad hillsides; the shyer chamois can occasionally be glimpsed in the national parks.

Venice at a Glance

Best Times To Visit

There are no quiet times to visit Venice between Easter and October. Even in winter, the city can be busy, especially at Christmas and New Year, and during February, when crowds flock in for the Lenten Carnival. If you are lucky, the winter months (Nov–Jan) can be delightful, but fog, rain and biting cold winds like the *bora* may blight your stay. *Acque alte* (surge tides, when parts of the city flood) occur with increasing frequency between the autumn and spring equinoxes. Day-trippers arrive in thousands during July and August, but temperatures and humidity levels are uncomfortable, and the canals can be smelly. Many Venetians choose to leave the city then, and central shops, restaurants and other businesses may close for annual holidays. The Lido beaches and hotels, however, are at their busiest in this period. Spring and autumn months have the best weather, and are regarded as high season; accommodation is expensive and hard to find if not booked well ahead.

Getting There

Venice is accessible by air, road, rail and sea (for details, *see* Travel Tips, page 122–123). The main international **airport** in Venice is Marco Polo, and an alternative arrival point is Treviso, about 30km (19 miles) north of Venice.

Getting Around

There are two ways to get around central Venice: **walk**, or take a **boat**. Distances are not great within the centre, but few land routes run 'as the crow flies'. You will inevitably get lost in a maze of streets – part of the Venetian experience. Yellow **tourist signs** can be found along the main routes, indicating 'Per San Marco', 'Per Rialto', 'Per Accademia', and so on. Comfortable, robust footwear is essential, especially in autumn and winter when low-lying areas periodically flood (listen for the warning sirens). Get hold of a clear, detailed city map. Many versions are available in hotels and tourist offices (some free), but they vary greatly in quality. Venice's main mode of transport is the ***vaporetto***. These hefty, diesel-powered water-buses bustle inelegantly but efficiently all round central Venice, stopping frequently. Slightly sleeker *motoscafi* and larger *motonavi* boats operate on longer routes round the lagoon. Collect an up-to-date boat transport map on your arrival; the numbered routes change periodically. Some operate seasonally, others only at night. No 1 (the *Accelerato*) plies the Grand Canal, stopping at every station between the Lido and Piazzale Roma, and crossing sides often. Take this route at least once, as it gives the best views of waterfront palaces. *Vaporetti* run fairly frequently (every 10–20 min during the day) and are easy to use once you get the hang of them, even with push-chairs or wheelchairs. Staff are always ready to help, but they don't waste time on dawdlers, so look sharp as you get on and off. Avoid taking the elegant mahogany **water-taxi** motor-boats, which are expensive. If you simply want to cross the Grand Canal, and aren't near a bridge, take a ***traghetto***, one of seven or eight ferry gondola routes which ply from specially signed piers. Fares are cheap; pay as you alight. Tips are not expected. Some *traghetti* operate for limited hours. Don't confuse *traghetti* with the excursion **gondolas**, which go from separate stands. These are a romantic but expensive way to see the city; negotiate a price before you set off.

Where to Stay

San Marco

Luxury

Gritti Palace, campo Santa Maria del Giglio 2467, tel: 041 794611, fax: 041 5200942. Doge Gritti's splendid 16th-century palazzo makes for an elegant, if very expensive, stay in a prime canal location.

Mid-range

Concordia, calle Larga 367, tel: 041 5206866, fax: 041 5206775. This claims to be the only hotel in Venice overlooking St Mark's Square; entrance hall cascades and flower-tubs make a soothing approach.

Venice at a Glance

Flora, off via XXII Marzo 2283, tel: 041 5205844, fax: 041 5228217. Charming family-run place, central, with garden. Venetian-style furnishings.
Kette, piscina San Moisè 2053, tel: 041 5207766, fax: 041 5228964. Stylish, in a quiet but central canalside location.
Santo Stefano, campo Santo Stefano 2957, tel: 041 5200166, fax: 041 5224460. Tall building on a lively square, with refurbished public areas.
Saturnia, via XXII Marzo 2398, tel: 041 5208377, fax: 041 5207131. Converted palazzo with rich furnishings, once owned by a Venetian admiral.
Violino d'Oro, campiello Barozzi 2091, tel: 041 2770841, fax: 041 2771001. Tastefully furnished hotel on a square, close to St Mark's.

Budget
Ai Do Mori, calle Larga 658, tel: 041 5204817, fax: 041 5205328. Spotless, with no public areas; breakfast isn't included in room rates, so you are free to enjoy local cafés.
San Fantin, campiello La Fenice 1930A, tel/fax: 041 5231401. Simple, family-run place in characterful building near Fenice opera house.

Castello

Luxury
Danieli, riva degli Schiavoni 4196, tel: 041 5226480, fax: 041 5200208. Sumptuous palace overlooking lagoon; the annexe is an afterthought.
Gabrielli Sandwirth, riva degli Schiavoni 4110, tel: 041 5231580, fax: 041 5209455. Upmarket waterfront palazzo hotel distinguished by family owners and a rooftop terrace.
Londra Palace, riva degli Schiavoni 4171, tel: 041 5200533, fax: 041 5225032. Lavish place with superb views, Biedermeier furnishings, original paintings and jacuzzi tubs.
Metropole, riva degli Schiavoni 4149, tel: 041 5205044, fax: 041 5223679. Lovely waterfront views grace this smart but unstuffy place, along with antiques and cabinets full of *objets d'art*.

Mid-range
Santa Marina, campo Santa Marina 6068, tel: 041 5239202, fax: 041 5200907. A buttercup yellow building on a quiet square, well run with good-quality furnishings. Favoured by numerous tour operators.
Scandinavia, campo Santa Maria Formosa 5240, tel: 041 5223507, fax: 041 5235232. Part of a major international consortium, but family-run. Handsome décor, excellent location for sightseeing.

Budget
Bucintoro, riva degli Schiavoni 2135, tel: 041 5223240, fax: 041 5235224. Simple *pensione* with superb waterfront views, close to the Naval Museum.
La Residenza, campo Bandiera e Moro 3608, tel: 041 5285315, fax: 041 5238859. Venetian Gothic façade dominates an atmospheric square. The rooms of this 15th-century palace are being upgraded.
Nuevo Teson, riva degli Schiavoni 3980/81, tel: 041 5229929, fax: 041 5285335. Tucked into a tiny *campiello* just off the waterfront esplanade near the Arsenale *vaporetto* stop, this unpretentious place is welcoming and inexpensive; the excellent Al Covo restaurant is just outside.

Cannaregio

Luxury
Grand Hotel dei Dogi, fondamenta Madonna dell'Orto 3500, tel: 041 2208111, fax: 041 722278. Secluded chain hotel in a former embassy building. Large, lovely grounds stretch to a private landing stage. Exquisite 18th-century style furnishings.

VENICE	J	F	M	A	M	J	J	A	S	O	N	D
AVERAGE TEMP. °F	43	46	54	63	70	77	81	81	76	66	54	46
AVERAGE TEMP. °C	6	8	12	17	21	25	27	27	24	19	12	8
HOURS OF SUN DAILY	4	5	6	7	9	10	12	10	7	5	4	3
RAINFALL in	2.3	1.5	2.9	3	2.8	2.8	1.4	1.9	2.8	2.6	2.9	2.1
RAINFALL mm	58	39	74	77	72	73	37	48	71	66	75	54
DAYS OF RAINFALL	6	6	7	9	8	8	7	7	5	7	9	8

Venice at a Glance

Mid-range

Giorgione, Santi Apostoli 4587, tel: 041 5225810, fax: 041 5239092. Renovated palazzo hotel, extensive public rooms and courtyard garden.
Locanda Ai Santi Apostoli, strada Nuova 4391, tel: 041 5212612, fax: 041 5212611. Near the Rialto, a secluded guesthouse with Grand Canal views from a peaceful lounge.

Budget

Locanda Leon Bianco, corte Leon Bianco 5629, tel: 041 5233572, fax: 041 2416392. A famous historic inn; some imaginatively decorated rooms face the Grand Canal.

Santa Croce/San Polo

Mid-range

Locanda Ovidius, calle del Sturion 677 A, tel: 041 5237970, fax: 041 5204101. Classically furnished little hotel in 18th-century style, with first-floor views of the Rialto.
Locanda Sturion, calle del Sturion 679, tel: 041 5236243, fax: 041 5228378. Above the Locanda Ovidius, this B&B has more stairs, but better views.
San Cassiano, Ca' Favretto, calle Rosa 2232, tel: 041 5241768, fax: 041 721033. Water-taxis drop you at this charming little palace. Elegant, though reception can be cool.
San Simon Ai Due Fanali, campo San Simeon Profeta 946, tel: 041 718490, fax: 041 718344. In old church *scuola*, near bus and rail stations.
Santa Chiara/Residenza Parisi, piazzale Roma 548, tel: 041 5206955, fax: 041 5228799. Waterfront views and handy road connections compensate for the bus station setting. Parking space.

Dorsoduro

Mid-range

Accademia Villa Maravege, fondamenta Bollani 1058, tel: 041 5237846, fax: 041 5239152. Elegant mansion with gardens in prime location.
American, San Vio 628, tel: 041 5204733, fax: 041 5204048. A welcoming place, first-floor breakfast terrace, pretty Italianate furnishings.

Budget

Agli Alboretti, rio Terrà Foscarini 884, tel: 041 5230058, fax: 041 5210158. Small canalside hotel with shady terrace.
Antico Capon, campo Santa Margherita 3004 B, tel/fax: 041 5285292. Clean *pensione* with helpful owner. Instead of an in-house breakfast, a voucher scheme lets you try some cafés; there's a good pizzeria (separately managed) downstairs.
Galleria, campo della Carità 878 A, tel: 041 5232489, fax: 041 5204172. Decorated in an opulent old-fashioned style, a B&B with Grand Canal views.
La Calcina, Fondamenta Zattere 780, tel: 041 5206466, fax: 041 5227045. John Ruskin stayed here in the 1890s; inside it's cosy and friendly. Waterfront terrace.

Islands

Luxury

Cipriani & Palazzo Vendramin, Giudecca 10, tel: 041 5207744, fax: 041 5207745. Glamorous haunt of the super-rich in palatial grounds; huge swimming pool.
Des Bains, lungomare Marconi 17, Lido, tel: 041 5265921, fax: 041 5260113. Setting for Mann's *Death in Venice* and the subsequent Visconti film, this *belle époque* pile presides over the Lido's Adriatic seafront.
Westin Excelsior, lungomare Marconi 41, Lido, tel: 041 5260201, fax: 041 5267276. Some guests of this Byzantine fantasy are as glamorous as its architecture, especially at Film Festival time. Palatial 5-star.

Where to Eat

San Marco

Luxury

Caffè Florian, piazza San Marco 56–59, tel: 041 5285338. An espresso here costs more than anywhere in Venice, so get your money's worth and spend time in this coffee house, listening to the band and watching the world go by. Closed Wed in winter.
Do Forni, calle degli Specchieri 457/468, tel: 041 5232148. A smart and pricey place with exemplary service and impressive clientele. One section replicates an Orient Express dining-car.
Gran Caffè Quadri, piazza San Marco 120, tel: 041 5289299. Florian's rival across the Piazza is ever-so-slightly

Venice at a Glance

cheaper – a haunt of Austrian officers during the occupation of Venice. The restaurant upstairs is for serious splurging only. Closed Mon in winter.
Harry's Bar, calle Vallaresso 1323, tel: 041 5285777. The legendary watering hole made famous by Hemingway and others. Hideously pricey, but for some a quintessential Venetian experience. Wonderful *carpaccio* and home-made pasta.
La Caravella, calle Larga XXII Marzo 2397/2402, tel: 041 5208901. *Nouvelle cuisine* and bravura international fare in a nautical setting in the Saturnia Hotel. Closed Wed.

Mid-range
Al Theatro, campo San Fantin 1917, tel: 041 5221052. Near the ill-starred Fenice opera house. Outside tables overlook a square. Elegant interior. Full meals, authentic pizza and *cichetti*. Roof garden; piano bar. Closed Mon in winter.
Gelateria Paolin, campo Santo Stefano 2962, tel: 041 5225576. Fine home-made ice cream, open till 22:00.
Osteria Ai Assassini, rio Terrà dei Assassini 3695, tel: 041 5287986. Choice of wines, beers, snacks and light meals in a rustic setting. Closed Sun.

Budget
Bar Al Campanile, Merceria 310, tel: 041 5221491. Snack bar near St Mark's and Rialto; try the *tramezzini* or *panini* chased with a spritzer.

Castello
Luxury
Al Covo, campiello della Pescaria 3968, tel: 041 5223812. Good cooking, cosy restaurant just off the Riva degli Schiavoni. Closed Wed and Thur.

Mid-range
Al Mascaron, calle Lunga Sta M Formosa 5525, tel: 041 5225995. An old-fashioned *osteria* serving good wines and snacks, plus a range of fish specials. Closed Sun.
Corte Sconta, calle del Pestrin 3886, tel: 041 5227024. So tucked away in a tiny alley it's a wonder anyone finds it, but book ahead to avoid disappointment. The fish specials draw crowds. Closed Mon.

Budget
Aciughetta, campo Santi Filippo e Giacomo 4357, tel: 041 5224292. Bar-cum-trattoria with lots of outdoor tables; central, popular. Closed Wed.
Al Vecio Canton, calle Corona 4738 A, tel: 041 5285176. An attractive trattoria offering enormous wood-fired pizzas, Venetian specialities and counter *cichetti*. Closed Tue.
Rosa Salva, campo Santi Giovanni e Paolo 6779, tel: 041 5227949. Several branches of this *dolcibar* chain exist in the city; serves lovely ice cream at tables overlooking the basilica.
Trattoria Alla Rivetta, Ponte San Provolo 4625, tel: 041 5287302. Popular for its fishy *cichetti* (snacks). Closed Mon.

Cannaregio
Luxury
Fiaschetteria Toscana, salizzada San Giovanni Crisostomo 5719, tel: 041 5285281. Good Venetian cuisine and extensive wine list. Closed Tue.

Mid-range
Cantina Vecia Carbonera, strada Nova 2348, tel: 041 710376. Wine bar serving gourmet snacks and sandwiches. Live jazz, late opening some nights. Closed Mon.
Osteria Anice Stellato, fondamenta de la Sensa 3272, tel: 041 720744. A civilized canalside restaurant popular with locals in an untouristy part of town. Good home cooking. Closed Mon.
Palazzina, ponte delle Guglie 1509, tel: 041 717725. A casually stylish trattoria serving pizzas, pasta and seafood. Lively but relaxing, it pulls in a youngish crowd. Service on the leisurely side. Closed Wed.
Trattoria La Colonna, campiello del Pestrin 5329, tel: 041 5229641. Excellent and reasonably priced place serving mainly fish in a quiet corner not far from Fondamenta Nuove. Closed Mon.

Budget
Caffè Costarica, rio Terrà di San Leonardo 1563, tel: 041 716371. Renowned for its home-roasted coffee, this place proffers definitive espresso and a good line in iced coffee (*frappé*). Closed Sun.

Venice at a Glance

Enoteca Boldrin, salizzada San Canciano 5550, tel: 041 5237859. One of the city's best self-service wine bars, spacious, bright and authentic. Pasta snacks and a big choice of wines by the glass or bottle.
Gam Gam, sottoportico di Ghetto Vecchio, tel: 041 715284. Interesting Levant and Jewish cooking (chicken soup, of course, plus latkes and schnitzels), in bustling modern café setting. Closed Sat.
I Quattro Rusteghi, campo Ghetto Novo 2888, tel: 041 715160. A trim café serving snacks and light meals near the Jewish Museum, though (unlike Gam Gam) not strictly kosher. Try the apple cake.
Osteria dalla Vedova (also known as Ca' d'Oro), calle del Pistor 3912, tel: 041 5285324. Ancient and characterful bar serving typical Venetian *ombra e cichetti* snacks and full meals at tables. Always popular. Closed Sun am and Thur.

Santa Croce/San Polo

LUXURY

Da Fiore, calle del Scaleter 2202, tel: 041 731308. Small, intimate place priding itself on its Venetian ways with seafood. Closed Sun and Mon.

MID-RANGE

Do Mori, calle dei Do Mori 429, tel: 041 5225401. One of the oldest and best *bacari* in the city. Amazing selection of wines and *cichetti*, but nowhere to sit down. Closed Sun.
Trattoria Alla Madonna, calle della Madonna 594, tel: 041 5223824. Acclaimed traditional fish restaurant in a side-alley near the Rialto. A sociable, bustling place at lunchtimes. Closed Wed/Jan.

BUDGET

Alle Oche, calle del Tintor 1459, tel: 041 5241161. Wide range of delicious, inexpensive pizzas draws queues of young folk. Cheerful atmosphere. Closed Mon in winter.
Birreria Snack Bar Alla Filovia, fondamenta Santa Chiara 519, no telephone. If you're waiting for a bus or *vaporetto* at Piazzale Roma, try this friendly, spacious snack bar. Well-filled sandwiches or *cichetti* with a glass of wine or beer cost much less here than in fancier parts of town.
Pizzeria d'Asporto/ Gelateria Millevoglie, salizzada San Rocco 3034, tel: 041 5244667. Wood-fired pizzas one side, mouth-watering ice cream the other – good for a snack after tackling the Frari. *Acqua alta* boardwalks make useful 'picnic tables' in the rainy season. Open till late.

Dorsoduro

MID-RANGE

Gelateria Nico, fondamenta alle Zattere 922, tel: 041 5225293. Waterfront views make Nico's ice cream a pricey treat, but the *gianduiotto* house special (hazelnut, chocolate and cream) is delicious.

BUDGET

Causin, campo Santa Margharita 2996, tel: 041 5236091. Home-made ice cream since 1928. Closed Sat.
Margaret Duchamp, campo Santa Margherita 3019, tel: 041 5286255. Cool camp café on agreeable square. Stylish modern décor. Good snacks; open until the small hours.
Trattoria Ai Cugnai, rio Terrà San Vio 857, tel: 041 5289238. The motherly ladies who run the place will give your spaghetti a stir if you seem to be having trouble with it. A simple, unassuming, family place, handy for the art galleries. Closed Mon.

Islands

LUXURY

Harry's Dolci, Giudecca 773, tel: 041 5224844. A cheaper way of sampling a Bellini, this offshoot of Harry's Bar has a waterfront terrace and exemplary service. The chocolate cake defies description.
Locanda Cipriani, Torcello, tel: 041 730150. This deceptively simple hostelry makes a relaxing lunchtime stop near Torcello's wonderful churches. Shady terrace tables, rustic dining rooms. Closed Tue.

MID-RANGE

Busa Alla Torre, campo Santo Stefano 3, Murano, tel: 041 739662. Charming restaurant with a colonnaded loggia and big white parasols opposite San Pietro Martire; good Venetian cooking, especially fish.

Venice at a Glance

Cip's, fondamenta San Giovanni 10, Giudecca, tel: 041 5207744. A recent Cipriani venture combining informal dining with elegance – the pontoon terrace of a grill restaurant, salad bar, pizzeria and patisserie offers non-residents a glimpse of the luxury hotel's exclusivity. Try the speciality: hot chocolate.
Ponte del Diavolo, fondita Borgognoni 10/11, Torcello, tel: 041 730401. *Osteria* with fishy main courses and home-made puddings and cakes for lunchtime visitors. Terrace.
Trattoria Da Romano, via Baldassare Galuppi 221, Burano, tel: 041 730030. This handsome townhouse provides a comfortable vantage point for Burano streetlife. Terrace tables, lots of space inside its dining room. Prompt, courteous service. Closed Tue.

Budget

Los Murales, fondamenta delle Zitelle 68/70/71, Giudecca, tel: 041 5230004. A taste of Tex-Mex on the waterfront near Zitelle. Macho nachos and chimichanga, with tequila or a margarita. Closed Wed.

Entertainment

Concerts, exhibitions, lectures and arty happenings abound. For listings information, get the latest edition of the bilingual free magazine *Un Ospite di Venezia* (A Guest in Venice) from hotels, tourist offices and newsagents. Other publications are the tourist office magazines *Leo* (monthly) and *Venice Pocket* (quarterly). Events can also be booked through hotels, at the Venice Pavilion, or in travel and tourist agencies. For major productions, go to the box office and book in person.
Music: Classical concerts are held in churches or palaces, sometimes more memorable for their settings than the quality of the performances: La Pietà, Frari, Scuola Grande di San Rocco, Palazzo Querini-Stampalia, even the courtyard of the Doge's Palace.
Opera: Until Teatro La Fenice is restored, Venetian opera-lovers have to go to the marquee tents of the Palafenice in Tronchetto. Ballet and concerts are also staged here. The box office is in Campo San Luca (tel: 041 5210161). Verona's Arena holds its international opera festival in Aug/Sept, and occasional pop or rock concerts at other times of year.
Film: Two of Venice's most popular cinemas are in Dorsoduro (the Accademia, calle Contarini Corfu 1018) and San Marco (the Ritz, calle dei Segretaria 617). Open-air screenings are held in Campo San Polo in summer. Most films are dubbed into Italian; original-version art-house movies are shown occasionally. Tickets for the Lido's prestigious international film festival are hard to obtain.
Theatre: Venice's main theatre, Teatro Goldoni (situated at calle Goldoni 4650b, tel: 041 5205422), puts on Italian classics from Nov–June.
Nightlife: There are relatively few nightclubs, discos or late-night bars in the city centre – the big club scene is on the mainland, in Mestre, or in the summer beach resorts like Lido di Jesolo. Some smart hotels and restaurants have piano bars. There are a few discreet music bars, for example:
Caffè Blue, salizzada San Pantalon 3778, Dorsoduro, tel: 041 5237227. Student bar with board games; live music on Fri (closed Sun).
Casanova Disco Café, lista di Spagna 158a, Cannaregio, tel: 041 2750199. Genre music (salsa, rock and wave, etc.) Wed–Sat.
Fiddler's Elbow, strada Nova 3847, Cannaregio, tel: 041 5239930. Best known of Venice's Irish music pubs.
Paradiso Perduto, fondamenta della Misericordia 2540, Cannaregio, tel: 041 720581. Live and piped music.
Piccolo Mondo, San Marco 1056a, Dorsoduro, tel: 041 5200371. Intimate disco catering for all tastes.
Old Well Pub, corte Canal 656, Campo de la Lana, Santa Croce, tel: 041 5242760. Lively bar with good beer.
Casinos: Venice's municipal casino occupies the Grand Canal palace where Wagner died (Palazzo Vendramin-Calergi, Cannaregio, tel: 041 5297111). Dress up and take your passport.

Venice at a Glance

Shopping

Many shops act as outlets for the specialist craft industries for which Venice is famous, especially marbled stationery, Murano glass and carnival masks. Some are workshops where visitors can watch the creative process in action. The fashion and textile industries are another great mainstay all over the Veneto. Many big Italian designer labels can be found in the smart shopping streets near St Mark's Square. Around **Via Larga XXII Marzo** you'll find Versace, Armani, Valentino and Bulgari; along the **Mercerie** and the **Calle dei Fabbri** lie high-street names like Benetton or Max & Co, and the big department store **Coin**, where stylish but less stratospherically priced clothing is found. Rich fabrics line the window displays of many specialist retailers: velvets and brocades, fine lace and pleated silks. Leatherware is another speciality: elegant, expensive shoes you could never sensibly wear in an *acqua alta* rub along with bags, belts and wallets. At the other end of the quality spectrum lie the market stalls of the **Strada Nova**, the trinket shops of the **Riva degli Schiavoni**, and street traders touting Chanel and Prada lookalike luggage off the pavements. Antique and bric-a-brac dealers ply their trade from suave premises or back-street rooms, and sometimes from flea markets in **Campo San Maurizio**. Food shopping is a pleasure in Venice. The **Rialto** is just one of many colourful markets in the city's *campi*, *calli* and *canale*. Cakes and biscuits, cheeses and salamis, sweets and chocolates, wines and grappa make lovely presents. Most shops accept credit cards or travellers' cheques for significant purchases. English is widely spoken.

Tours and Excursions

Lots of travel agents, tour companies and private guides advertise excursions in and around Venice. The tourist office can provide a list of reputable firms. The **Associazione Guide Turistiche**, calle Cassellaria 5327, Castello, tel: 041 5210762, is an official guide co-operative offering tailor-made tours in many languages (minimum charge). Rates for authorized guides and gondoliers are advertised in *Un Ospite di Venezia*, but these are negotiable. **American Express** is one of the best-known tour organizers for English-speaking visitors. Its office is at salizzada San Moisè 1471, off St Mark's Square, tel: 041 5200844. Escorted sightseeing tours of the city depart daily from here, and from the **Thomas Cook** office at riva del Ferro 5126, San Marco (near Rialto Bridge). **Oltrex** is a well-established agency, easily found along the Riva degli Schiavoni in Castello (tel: 041 5242840). Gondola rides can be booked, as well as longer trips to the lagoon islands, Veneto cities and the Palladian villas of the Brenta Canal. Some excursions to Murano and Burano place heavy emphasis on visiting glass factories or lace shops, and are poor value. It is not difficult to organize independent trips by public transport at a fraction of the cost, even if you don't speak Italian. A fine escorted tour is the **Itinerari Segreti** (Secret Trails) of the Doge's Palace, daily at 10:00 and 12:00 (tel: 041 5224951).

Useful Contacts

Venice Tourist Board, tel: 041 5298711.
Marco Polo Airport, tel: 041 2609260 for flight times and general information.
Santa Lucia Station, tel: 1478 88 088 for regional rail information.
ACTV (*Azienda Consorzio Trasporti Veneziano*), Piazzale Roma, tel: 041 5287886 for information on local public transport (boats and buses).
Radio Taxi, tel: 041 936222. For mainland road journeys.
Venetian Hoteliers Association (Associazione Veneziana Albergatori), branches at Marco Polo Airport, Piazzale Roma (car-park building), and Santa Lucia railway station. Reservations on arrival.
Disabled visitors, tel: 041 976435.
Venice's official **website** is www.venetia.it

Travel Tips

Tourist Information

The Italian State Tourist Office (ENIT) has overseas offices in many major European cities, including London, and also in Canada (Montreal) and the USA (Chicago, Los Angeles, New York). It is represented in Australia (Sydney) by the Italian Chamber of Commerce. In Venice, several branches of **Azienda di Promozione Turistica** (APT) provide local information on the city and its immediate surroundings, but little about the more distant parts of the Veneto. There is one central telephone number: 041 5298711. Main tourist offices are in or near St Mark's Square: at piazza San Marco 71 and in the recently opened Venice Pavilion, by the waterfront gardens (Giardini Ex Reali). The latter is also a bookshop, box office and internet point (tel: 041 5225150). Smaller branches are at Marco Polo airport (arrivals hall), and at Santa Lucia station. There is a summer-only office on the Lido (Gran Viale 6a). In high season, additional information booths (*punti informativi*) are set up at strategic points.

Entry Requirements

All visitors require a valid passport. Visas are not required for citizens of the EU, Switzerland, the USA, Canada, Japan, Israel, Australia or New Zealand for stays of under three months, but most others will need one (check with an Italian embassy or consulate before departure).

Customs

EU travellers incur no extra tax on reasonable quantities of goods bought duty- and tax-paid within the EU. Maximum quantities appropriate for personal consumption or gifts are currently 800 cigarettes; 10 litres of spirits and 90 litres of wine. Limits for non-EU visitors are: 400 cigarettes or 200 small cigars or 100 large cigars or 500g tobacco; 1 litre of spirits or 2 litres of wine; 50g perfume or 250g cologne.

Health Requirements

No vaccinations are required to enter Italy except from areas known to be infected with cholera or yellow fever. All EU citizens and some other nationals with reciprocal health agreements are entitled to emergency medical treatment on presentation of the appropriate documentation (an E111 form for EU visitors). Adequate medical insurance is recommended for all travellers.

Getting There

By air: Direct flights operate to Venice from many European cities, but there are no direct intercontinental flights. Marco Polo airport is 10km (6 miles) north of the city on the edge of the lagoon. It receives international and domestic traffic, including scheduled flights by Alitalia, Italy's national carrier, or Go, the low-cost airline. Treviso airport, 30km (19 miles) north of Venice, handles charter and low-cost flights such as Ryanair's. Verona also has an international airport offering easy access to the Veneto, Lake Garda and the Dolomites.

By rail or coach: Road and rail links to Venice cross the lagoon via the Ponte della Libertà. Santa Lucia is the main railway station, in Cannaregio at the head of the Grand Canal. It has regular, efficient connections to many Italian centres (Milan, Florence, Pisa, Rome, etc.) and

to the European rail network. The luxury trans-European Venice–Simplon Orient Express from London via Paris, Zürich and Verona stops at Santa Lucia. Opposite the railway station (in Santa Croce) is the bus and coach terminal, Piazzale Roma, where local and long-distance buses stop. No vehicular traffic is permitted in the city beyond this point.
By car: If you have a private car, you will have to leave it in a car park on the mainland (e.g. near the airport and in Mestre) or central Venice (huge multi-storey parking sheds dominate Piazzale Roma and the island of Tronchetto). Parking is expensive and hard to find.
By sea: Venice is a popular port of call for Mediterranean cruise ships, and on certain scheduled Adriatic ferry routes too. Arriving by sea is the most romantic way to reach the city.
Getting into the city: Marco Polo and Treviso airports are linked by regular bus routes to Piazzale Roma, and by taxis too. Some airlines and operators provide free coach or minibus transfers into the city. From Marco Polo, an expensive way to Venice is by the scheduled Alilaguna hydrofoil (*motoscafo*) service across the lagoon to St Mark's Square (buy your ticket in the arrivals hall). Try this route, one way at least, for a memorable ride. Water-taxis are faster, but prohibitively expensive unless you travel in a group of half a dozen or so. Be especially wary of unlicensed water-taxis (which don't show a clear number-plate); these are notorious for overcharging.

What to Pack

Dress reasonably smartly in the evenings. But no one would totter round cobbled streets or jump on and off *vaporetti* in tight skirts or high heels. Take smart casual clothes and comfortable walking shoes. A scarf or shawl is useful for covering arms or shoulders in churches. For summer, take cool cottons, sunglasses, sunscreen and a hat or scarf. Venice can be chilly in spring or autumn, and very cold in winter. Take waterproofs, an umbrella, insect repellent, an antihistamine cream and a light fly swat. Small binoculars are handy for campanile views or bird-watching. Take oodles of film. Whatever you pack, you'll want to bring a lot home; leave space or take an extra bag.

Money Matters

Until Euro notes and coins are introduced in 2002, the **currency** in Italy is still the lira, abbreviated as 'L'. Notes are in denominations of L1000, L2000, L5000, L10,000, L50,000 and L100,000, coins in values of L5, L10, L50, L100, L200 and L500. The larger coins are good for tips, public telephones, and lighting up churches. You can **change money** at the airport and station, but banks usually offer the best rate. There are many banks around San Marco and the Rialto. Hotels usually offer poorer rates. American Express or Thomas Cook **travellers' cheques** can be changed commission-free at their respective offices in Venice.
American Express: salizzada San Moisè 1471, San Marco;
Thomas Cook: branches in Piazza San Marco and at Riva del Ferro, near Rialto Bridge.
Major **credit cards** (Visa or Eurocard/Access) are accepted in hotels, tourist shops and restaurants, but cash is preferred. Don't proffer them for museum admission, or in small bars, cafés and food stores. You can use credit cards to obtain cash in banks displaying the right sign.
Tipping is widely expected, despite the 10–15 per cent service charge often included in restaurant bills. A few coins will do for drinks ordered at a bar, or for cloakroom attendants. L1000 or 2000 notes are useful for chambermaids, usherettes, porters, church custodians and so forth. Gondoliers and tour guides expect rather more.
Non-EU residents can claim back **VAT** on goods purchased in Italy. Complete and keep the relevant documents and obtain a customs stamp as you leave the country. Claim your refund within three months of return.

Accommodation

Venice's 200-plus hotels range from basic to some of the most sybaritic in the world. Within a few paces, you can find deluxe waterfront palazzi, business hotels, and eccentric family *pensioni*. Historic mansions may be renovated with stylish décor and fine plumbing, or show signs of dilapidation that may strike you as dismal. Whatever their quality, hotels are rarely underbooked. The mismatch of supply and demand means astronomical **prices** during any period considered 'high season' (almost year-round in some places). Jan and Mar are fairly quiet; May–Jun and Sep–Oct are very popular, while the Lido is busiest in Jul–Aug. Carnival time (Feb) is a sell-out months in advance. Expect to pay up to 30 per cent more for accommodation in Venice than anywhere else in Italy. Even a modest *pensione*, *albergo* or *locanda* can command heart-stopping tariffs, especially if it has canal views. To be sure of a reservation, **book** well ahead (at least two months) and take written confirmation with you. Internet or fax bookings, with credit card, are more reliable than the post. Package holidays are often cheaper than independent bookings. Hotels are **graded** from one to five stars, with a luxury category for a few very exclusive places. The tourist office's annually updated list of registered accommodation indicates price ranges. Prices vary seasonally. Few small hotels have restaurants, but most include breakfast (generally poor value compared with local bars or cafés). Weekend supplements may be charged. Most areas of Venice are safe and accessible, but **location** is important. Hotels are scattered throughout the central *sestieri*. San Marco and Castello have some plush hotels (several converted palazzi face the Grand Canal). Cheaper (often seedier) places cluster round the bus and railway stations in Cannaregio and Santa Croce. Dorsoduro has quiet, charming canalside hotels. Few lagoon islands have accommodation, apart from Giudecca and the Lido, which boast some of Venice's most exclusive establishments. Despite the lack of conventional traffic, some waterfront palaces are noisy: clanging bells, revving boat engines, garbage collections, even serenading gondoliers. Venetian postal addresses are fiendish; ensure you have a street name, a map reference and a landmark to help you find your hotel. Check out the nearest *vaporetto* stop, and consider how far you'll have to carry your luggage – or pay someone else to do it. Resist the temptation to save money by staying in Marghera or Mestre. These industrialized towns are no substitute for central Venice.

CONVERSION CHART

FROM	TO	MULTIPLY BY
Millimetres	Inches	0.0394
Metres	Yards	1.0936
Metres	Feet	3.281
Kilometres	Miles	0.6214
Square kilometres	Square miles	0.386
Hectares	Acres	2.471
Litres	Pints	1.760
Kilograms	Pounds	2.205
Tonnes	Tons	0.984

To convert Celsius to Fahrenheit: x 9 ÷ 5 + 32

If Venice is impossibly crowded or expensive, try somewhere like Treviso or Padua, with efficient public transport to the city. Serviced apartments are expensive, but **self-catering** is good value for families staying longer (a week is usually the minimum). The tourist office can advise on **budget accommodation**, like B&B in private homes with a family, student residences or youth hostels (the Ostello Venezia is at Giudecca 86, tel: 041 5238211). Many campsites, some with chalets or bungalows, straggle along the Adriatic coast.

Eating Out

Eating out can be expensive and cooking indifferent in many tourist-oriented restaurants. A stream of tourists has made some restaurants complacent. But standards are improving. With over 300 eateries, competition is fierce. Venetians tolerate no slackness or corner-cutting, so watch where the locals go. Places with a good reputation are full; in high season, always book ahead. Some of the most charming restaurants have waterfront views, tables in courtyard gardens, rooftop terraces or sunny squares. Check closing days. Meals are usually as follows: lunch (*pranzo*) 12:30–14:00; dinner (*cena*) 19:30–21:30. Few places stay open very late. Around San Marco or the railway station, the tyranny of the *menu turistico* (a dreary fixed-price affair, usually pasta with tomato sauce and wilted salad, followed by ice cream or fruit) reigns supreme. The attraction is the price-tag. Conventional menus are structured so that you often end up spending far more than you anticipated by the time cover, a tip and taxes have been added. Don't be intimidated if a menu suggests pasta can only be ordered as a 'first course'. You don't have to order an expensive fish or meat course. A meal consisting of a starter or salad, followed by a pasta dish, is acceptable in all but the smartest restaurants. There are other ways to save money. Family *trattorie* in more neighbourly parts of the city can be more fun, and better value, than fancier restaurants in commercialized areas. If you only want a snack, don't waste money on formal meals. Go to a self-service restaurant (*tavola calda*) or a wine bar (*enoteca*) where service charges aren't obligatory. Have snacks (*cichetti*) at atmospheric bars (*bacari*) and inns (*osterie*), or buy a sandwich or pastry from a takeaway snack bar. If you have a sweet tooth, you'll find the cake shops (*pasticcerie*) and bakeries irresistible. Find a good pizzeria with authentic wood-burning stove or a cheap-and-cheerful *spaghetteria* for a plate of pasta. It's easy to put together a delicious picnic of cheese, fruit, olives and cold cuts from market stalls and food shops near the Rialto.

Transport

Public transport is run by the Azienda del Consorzio Trasporti Veneziano (ACTV), with information offices in Piazzale Roma and in Corte dell'Albero, San Marco 3880.

Exploring the Veneto

By train: The main cities of the Veneto (Padua, Vicenza, Verona, Treviso) are easily accessible by rail from Santa Lucia station. Services are reliable and inexpensive. Trains are run by the Ferrovie dello Stato (FS). There are several categories: faster services like Inter City may incur fare supplements and seat reservation charges. First- and second-class tickets (*biglietti*) are sold for single (*andata*) or return (*andata e ritorno*) journeys. Validate your ticket in the platform machine before you travel, or you may get a fine.
By bus: From Piazzale Roma, regional bus routes radiate via the Ponte della Libertà to many towns and villages. Local services are operated by ACTV; further ones by ATVO (*Azienda Trasporti Veneto Orientale*) and others. Buy tickets at the bus station, newsstands or *tabacchi*.
Car rental: Many international firms have offices at Marco Polo and Treviso airports, Santa Lucia railway station and Piazzale Roma. You will need a valid driving licence and passport.

Business Hours

Banks: Mon–Fri 08:00–14:00. Exchange facilities are available for longer hours at Marco Polo airport, Santa Lucia station, etc.
Post Offices: Mon–Fri 08:00–13:30 (some also Sat am). Head office Mon–Sat 08:15–19:00.
Pharmacies: Mon–Fri 09:00–12:30, 16:00–20:00; Sat: 09:00–12:00 (area branches take turns to stay open 24hrs – local rosters posted on doors, and published in local papers or in *Un Ospite di Venezia*).
Shops and Businesses: Mon–Sat 09:00–12:30 or 13:00, 16:00–19:30. Larger stores and supermarkets stay open all day.
Tourist Offices: main office in St Mark's Square Mon–Sat 09:30–15:30.
Churches, galleries and museums: very variable; see individual entries or *Un Ospite di Venezia*. Some museums close on Mon.

Time

Italy is on Central European time (1 hour ahead of GMT in winter, 2 hours in summer).

Communications

The international **dialling code** for Italy is +39, followed by 041 for Venice. Cheap rates from Mon–Sat 22:00–08:00, all day Sunday. Orange **payphones**

USEFUL PHRASES

Yes, no • *si, no*
Good morning • *Buon giorno*
Good evening/night • *Buona sera/notte*
Hello/goodbye • *Ciao* (informal)
Please • *per favore*
Thank you very much • *mille grazie*
You're welcome • *prego*
I'm sorry • *mi dispiace*
May I get past? • *permesso*
I don't understand • *non capisco*
Do you speak English • *parla inglese?*
How much is it? • *quant'è?*
Where is...? • *dov'è...?*
My name is... • *mi chiamo...*
I would like... • *vorrei...*
Exit • *uscita*
Open • *aperto*
Closed • *chiuso*

PUBLIC HOLIDAYS

1 January • New Year's Day
6 January • Epiphany
March/April • Easter Monday
25 April • Liberation Day/ Feast of St Mark
1 May • Labour Day
15 August • Feast of the Assumption
1 November • All Saints' Day
8 December • Immaculate Conception
25 December • Christmas Day
26 December • Feast of St Stephen

can be found in public places, bars and restaurants. Some take coins (L100, L200, L500) or tokens (*gettoni*) worth L200; but many now take only credit cards or **phone cards** (*schede telefoniche*), available in post offices, *tabacchi* or shops and bars displaying the Telecom Italia logo. Call rates are high; those charged by hotels often extortionate. The main **post office** is in the Fondaco dei Tedeschi (San Marco). If not surcharged as 'espresso', post from Venice adds new meaning to the phrase 'snail mail'. A sprinkling of **cybercafés** now widens the city's horizons.

Electricity

Power in Italy is 220 volts AC, using mostly two-pin sockets. UK visitors require an adaptor; US visitors a voltage transformer. Be cautious if using sensitive electronic equipment; some foreign appliances may perform poorly and not all components are compatible.

Health Precautions

Visitors are unlikely to suffer more than a mild stomach upset, a touch of the sun and a few mosquito bites. Water is safe to drink unless marked *acqua non potabile*.

Health Services

A pharmacy (*farmacia*) has the standard green cross sign. Staff can dispense some useful medicines. Ask at your hotel if you need a doctor or dentist. Local health centres (*Unita Sanitaria Locale*) hold public clinics, but you need to book. For emergency treatment (*pronto soccorso*), dial **118** or go to a hospital casualty department. Ospedale Civile is at Campo Santi Giovanni e Paolo; tel: 041 5294517. Take your E111 or insurance forms and your passport, and keep the receipts for any bills you pay.

Personal Safety

Venice has an enviable reputation as the safest tourist city in Europe. Bad things can happen anywhere, but violence is rare. If you take sensible precautions with belongings and are reasonably streetwise, you are unlikely to suffer loss or injury.

Emergencies

General SOS tel: 113;
City Police tel: 112;
Fire tel: 115;
Ambulance tel: 118;
City hospital: tel: 041 5230000 or 041 5294517.

Etiquette

Thoughtless visitors who loiter in groups blocking narrow bridges do not endear themselves to local residents. During *acque alte* periods when the duckboards are out, behave sensibly and move along briskly in single file; splashing in the water is deplored. At *vaporetti* stations, allow disembarking passengers off before boarding. On *traghetti*, it is customary to stand rather than sit. Smoking is more prevalent in Italy than in some countries, but is prohibited on *vaporetti*.

GOOD READING

Dibdin, Michael (1994) Dead Lagoon. Faber, London
Goy, Richard (1997) *Venice: The City and its Architecture*. Phaidon, London
Holberton, Paul (1990) *Palladio's Villas*. John Murray, London
James, Henry (orig. 1902) *The Wings of the Dove*. Penguin, London
Mann, Thomas (1971, orig. 1921) *Death in Venice*. Penguin, London
McCarthy, Mary (1993, orig. 1956) *Venice Observed*. Penguin, London
Morris, Jan (1993, 3rd edn) *Venice*. Faber, London
Morris, Jan (1980) *The Venetian Empire: A Sea Voyage*. Penguin, London
Norwich, John Julius (1983) *A History of Venice*. Penguin, London
Ruskin, John (1853) *The Stones of Venice* (abridged by JG Links, 1960). Da Capo, London
Steer, John (1984) *A Concise History of Venetian Painting*. Thames & Hudson, London

INDEX

Note: Numbers in **bold** indicate photographs